Motivated
MINDS

Motivated
MINDS

Raising Children to Love Learning

Deborah Stipek, Ph.D., and Kathy Seal

AN OWL BOOK

Henry Holt and Company ▪ New York

Henry Holt and Company, LLC
Publishers since 1866
115 West 18th Street
New York, New York 10011

Henry Holt® is a registered trademark of
Henry Holt and Company, LLC.

Library of Congress Cataloging-in-Publication Data

Stipek, Deborah J., 1950–
  Motivated minds : raising children to love learning / Deborah Stipek and
Kathy Seal—1st ed.
      p.   cm.
  Includes bibliographical references and index.
  ISBN 0-8050-6395-1
  1. Motivation in education.   2. Education—Parent participation.   I. Title: Raising
children to love learning.   II. Seal, Kathy.   III. Title.
LB1065 .S83 2001
370.15'4—dc21   00-046197

Henry Holt books are available for special promotions and
premiums. For details contact: Director, Special Markets.

First Edition 2001

Designed by Kelly S. Too

Printed in the United States of America
3   5   7   9   10   8   6   4   2

Kathy: *To Zach, Jeff, and Jim, who understood, supported, and celebrated.*

Deborah: *To my parents, who always encouraged and never demanded, and my daughter—living proof that children can love learning.*

CONTENTS

AUTHORS' NOTE

To simplify our stories and include both our experiences, we have combined ourselves into one person, the "I" of our narrative. We also merged our children—Deborah's daughter, Meredith, and Kathy's sons, Zach and Jeff—into one literary family.

There are many references in this book to UES, the Corinne Seeds University Elementary School. UES is the laboratory school of UCLA, where innovative educational practices are developed, assessed, and disseminated. The school is committed to providing an educational program that promotes the joy of learning in children. Deborah was the director of UES from 1991 to 2000 and both Deborah's and Kathy's children attended the school.

ACKNOWLEDGMENTS

Kathy

Writing this book has been enormously enjoyable, not least because of the support of my family and friends, and their enthusiasm for the topic.

First I'd like to thank the trio of psychologists who were so generous with their time and from whom I always felt altruistic impulses as they explained their work unstintingly and sent copies of their papers, sharing pertinent personal anecdotes along the way: Carol Dweck, Richard Ryan, and Marty Covington, thanks for your research and your help. Jim Stigler, Wendy Grolnick, Sandra Graham, and Sharon Nelson-LeGall also contributed key interviews. I'm grateful as well to Angela Ebron and Sylvia Barsotti, Richard Atcheson and Nelson Algren Jr., who saw the value of these ideas, commissioning and editing gracefully my articles in *Lear's* and *Family Circle*.

A number of educators have also been quite helpful. Thanks to Sandy Stipianski of the NAEYC play caucus and Joe Sperling for their help with the chapter on play, and to Jeff Howard for the work of the Efficacy Institute and their "get-smart" formulation of Carol Dweck's work. Most especially I'd like to thank Betty Factor, Lucia Diaz, June Payne, Dr. Saundra Sperling, Rena Ellis, and the many others at the Mar Vista Family Center who practice the theories in this book every day, and have shown how to apply in particular the concept of autonomy to raising children. I appreciate as well the help of Phil Platzman and Steve Eisenberg in illuminating the playfulness of Richard Feynman.

I could not have coauthored this book without the interest and help of friends and fellow writers: Linda Marsa, who said, "Why don't you write a book?"; Barbara and Danny Sabbeth, who provided me a home in New York City and, more important, their love and encouragement; and my writers' group and good friends who traveled the book proposal and writing route with me, offering wise support and supplying fine anecdotes from their own lives when I asked: Julia Maher, Dorothy Chin, Barbara Beebe, Elizabeth Stanley, Gayle Pollard, Henry Unger, Armin and Mary Fields, and Leonia Kurgin. Hero medals go to Julia, Dorothy, and Barbara—the most highly educated typing crew ever— who unhesitatingly rotated at my computer during a dreadful deadline weekend when I was convinced (erroneously) that I was suffering from severe repetitive stress injury.

Several friends and relatives also took time out from their busy lives to read and comment most helpfully on the entire manuscript, from their points of view both professional and parental: Ann Shenkin, Susie Kaplan, Richard Cohen, and Margaret Lee. I'm very grateful for their thoughtful suggestions. Beth Howard also unselfishly smoothed my way.

Our agent Heide Lange has been invaluable. Thanks also to our editor, David Sobel, for his sharp and constructive critique, and to Heide and David, parents both, for understanding and believing in this project. To the crew at Holt—Maggie Richards, Elizabeth Shreve, David Shue, and Sarah Hutson—thanks for your expertise and hard work.

Crucial too were those "standing behind me"—my father and fellow author, Henry Shenkin; Reva Kaplan; and my siblings Budd, Bob, and Emily (my lawyer), who each assisted in a different way. I thank too my helpful and sweet laboratory subjects, Zach and Jeff, and my husband, Jim, for his unstinting support and love.

Deborah

Thanks also to Frances Forman, Janete Chun, and Rachel Longaker, who provided indispensable help.

Motivated
MINDS

Introduction

Have you ever said anything like this to your child?

"I know you're in the middle of building your block castle, but you'll just have to leave it for now and finish when we get back from the store."

Or:

"Will you *please* get off the Internet so someone else in this house can use the phone? I don't care if you haven't read everything there is on the Web about polar bears."

If comments like these sound familiar, it means you've seen your child intensely absorbed in work that demands brainpower. It means you've witnessed self-motivation up close and your child shows signs of loving learning.

Perhaps, however, your home sounds more like this one:

MOM: Jason, please get to your homework.

(A half-hour passes.)

DAD: Jason, have you started yet? It looks to me like all you're doing is staring into space.

(Fifteen minutes later.)

MOM *(voice rising)*: Jason, stop fiddling around right now. It's almost bedtime and you've barely started your homework! If you want to go to the basketball game Saturday, you better start studying, and I mean *now*!

(Jason slams his bedroom door angrily and plays a Rage Against the Machine *CD at maximum volume. Mom sinks to the couch, demoralized. Dad turns on* Jeopardy.*)*

MOM *(wailing)*: How long can this go on? I hate fighting every night.

DAD: Me too. I'm starting to dread coming home.

Every child is born with a desire to learn. Indeed, most children enter kindergarten excited about learning to read and write, and eager to know about the world around them.

Yet by the time they reach middle school (and often before), many of our children are like Jason. They look on learning as drudgery, not the exciting opportunity that propelled them when they were little. The idea that learning can be fun all but disappears—as illustrated by a boy who thanked me for my gift of *Tom Sawyer*, then added, "I'll read it later. I already did my book report for this semester."

So if you've noticed a lack of motivation in your child, you're not alone: research has shown that American children's love of learning declines steadily from third through ninth grade.[1]

It doesn't have to be that way.

Over the past thirty years, psychologists have conducted hundreds of studies that show what makes children *want* to learn. Their research tells us how to raise a child who is interested in academic work and even finds pleasure and joy in learning. It shows us how to raise children who seek intellectual challenges, and who plow on confidently even when the going gets tough.

I am going to show you how to raise just such an enthusiastic, life-long learner, but first we have to move beyond some ideas that research has shown are misguided.

For the past several decades, parents have been told that the best way to encourage kids to learn is to puff up their self-esteem by piling on rewards and praise. Grades and prizes have been considered the most effective tools for motivating children to study.

But psychologists have shown that raising eager learners is not simply a matter of making children "feel good." Indeed, the research I am going to share with you reveals how such a strategy can do damage.

What we have learned, instead, is that we need to raise children who feel competent, autonomous, and secure in their relationships to others. Kids will be self-motivated to learn when they feel capable and skilled, and confident of becoming more so; when they have some choice and control over their learning; and when they feel loved, supported, and respected by their parents. Children who love learning also believe that intelligence isn't fixed and inborn, but that they can get smarter by working hard.

I will show you how to nurture in your child these four essential components of loving learning. We will also examine why children learn so well through play, and how to encourage your child's natural drive toward competence.

Although this book focuses on children from babyhood through elementary school, its general principles and recommendations apply to children of all ages, and even to adults. Everyone can follow the self-motivation model you will read about in upcoming chapters: the cycle of working hard, persisting to overcome obstacles, and being energized to do more by the feelings of pleasure brought by newly gained confidence.

But maybe the notion of your child loving learning sounds to you like an impossible dream. Perhaps, like Jason's parents, you'd be satisfied if your child would simply take charge of his own homework. So, while we'll strive together for the ideal—a genuine love of learning—I am also going to show you how to raise a child who studies on his own, without monitoring, nagging, or threats of punishment.

Along the way, you will learn how to solve many of the common problems that children have with their schoolwork. I will show you how to prepare your young child to succeed in school, how to build your child's self-confidence and strengthen her persistence in the face of challenging work, and how to lessen her performance anxiety so she can concentrate on learning. Together we will raze the barriers to your child succeeding in school and enjoying learning.

Learning Better and Enjoying It More

But should you bother? What does it matter if your child *enjoys* learning, as long as she does her schoolwork?

It matters *a lot*. Researchers have shown decisively that when children study because they enjoy it, their learning is deeper, richer, and longer lasting. They are also more persistent, more creative, and more eager to do challenging work. There's an emotional payoff too: kids who *want* to learn feel less anxious and resentful than students coerced by bribes or threats, while achieving just as much or more.

"But I Want My Child to Score Well on Tests and Go to a Good College!"

You are probably also concerned about ensuring your child's success in the real world of report cards, standardized tests, and competitive admissions. The good news may seem paradoxical: research has shown that the indirect strategy of helping your child enjoy learning and see its value is the best way to improve your child's grades and raise her test scores.

This indirect strategy will also help you protect your child from the steep emotional price of the pressure to perform, which is mounting steadily today as tests take center stage in the politicized drive to improve our public schools. I'm going to help you cope with these testing demands while protecting your child from nail-biting anxiety and the emotional "turnoff" that are sure to follow if tests take precedence over learning.

The Good-Enough Parent

You'll find lots of practical suggestions in this book. But I don't expect you to follow them perfectly, for several reasons.

The first reason is illustrated by a well-intentioned book I once read. I don't remember the problem the book addressed, but I do remember throwing it down in disgust when it suggested that I talk like this to my children: "I'm wondering if your lost homework papers are your way of letting us know how you feel about us limiting your TV time?"

This is not that kind of book. I'm a working parent, perhaps like you. Many nights I'm too tired or preoccupied to be the sweet and patient Perfect Mother. Nor do I have all day to read *Treasure Island* to my son, write a three-act play based on the novel, and then sew costumes so we can act it out together. It's okay that I'm not perfect, and it's okay for you too. You don't have to be a licensed therapist, a millionaire with a household staff of twenty, or a Ph.D. / M.D./ M.B.A. to nurture your child's desire to learn. As the eminent British psychiatrist D. W. Winnicott used to say, kids don't need perfect parents. It's fine for you to be a "good-enough mother" (or father), who is "there" faithfully for your child and does what you can. No one can do more.

Furthermore, I may make a suggestion that you know for certain would not work with your child, perhaps because of her temperament. Or perhaps my strategy simply doesn't feel comfortable to you. This doesn't mean you are wrong, or that the research is mistaken. It simply means you need to adapt my suggestions to your own family. That's why parenting is more an art than a science. My advice provides solid guidelines, but you'll have to experiment to see what feels right and works best for you and your child.

Also, don't let the many strategies I suggest overwhelm you. If you can absorb the theme of this book and make its spirit your own, if you can follow a few of its tips, and if, above all, you let your child know that you value learning highly, that will be good enough. You'll give your family a healthy learning environment, and your child will stand a great chance of loving learning.

Raising children who *want* to learn is not a utopian dream or an unaffordable luxury. It's something every parent can achieve. It's also a key to improving American education, one that has been lost in our panic to increase achievement test scores. Imagine what it would be like if the majority of our children wanted to learn, plain and simple. Imagine if school-age kids enjoyed the expansion of their skills and knowledge the same way they enjoyed learning to recognize new letters, count to ten, ride a bike, or swim. They would be unstoppable, and our national quest to improve education would be infinitely easier.

So for your child's sake, and the nation's sake—read on.

I

Encouraging Your Child's
Love of Learning

It was 1947 and Richard Feynman was burned out. Work felt like drudgery to the twenty-nine-year-old physicist, and he feared he'd never make any important scientific discoveries. So Feynman decided to continue teaching, which he enjoyed. But as for theoretical physics, he told himself, he'd simply fool around with it.

"I'm going to play with physics," he thought, "whenever I want to, and without worrying about any importance whatsoever."[1]

A few days after that decision, Feynman was eating in the Cornell University cafeteria, when a student threw a plate toward him. (The Frisbee hadn't yet been invented.) As the dish traveled through the air, Feynman noticed that the red Cornell medallion on the rim of the white plate was spinning at a rate faster than the plate was wobbling. Calculating the motion of the rotating plate, he discovered that when the angle was slight, the medallion rotated twice as fast as the plate wobbled. "Hey, Feynman, that's pretty interesting," his colleague Hans Bethe said to him, "but what's the importance of it?"[2]

Feynman had no idea. He'd figured out the equation the way some-one else attacks a crossword puzzle or a Rubik's cube. Eighteen years later, however, Feynman would win the Nobel Prize for quantum elec-trodynamics—explaining, among other things, the peculiar "wob-bling" motion of electrons as they orbit the nucleus of an atom. This work of "figuring out the equations of wobbles," as he put it, had begun as play that day in the Cornell cafeteria.

How very eccentric Feynman was—and not only because his pre-ferred study nook when he later taught at Caltech in Pasadena was in the local topless bar. Feynman was unusual because he often pursued intellectual activities with no goal in mind other than his own pleasure. The prizewinning physicist had an extraordinarily high level of intrin-sic motivation, the desire to learn something "because you *want* to" rather than "because you *have* to."

What you may not realize is that *every* child is born with a healthy measure of this internal motivation to learn, a seedling that can blos-som into a full-fledged love of learning in school and in life.

Wired to Learn

Remember how busy your baby was when he wasn't sleeping or eat-ing? Looking, grabbing, dropping toys over the rail of the crib—babies are perpetual motion machines, programmed to explore and experi-ment in a relentless drive to learn about their world from the moment they enter it.

Your two-year-old's "I do it," or your three-year-old's endless string of "Why?" and "What's that?" (in my daughter's case, "Waas sat?") questions, or your four-year-old's repeated attempts to draw a dragon also reveal this inborn desire to learn. Although your five-year-old insisting on methodically tying her own shoes when you're late for work may seem self-centered or annoying, she's simply driven by a powerful innate force to master this new skill. The preteen whose

Tetris sounds drive you crazy as he determinedly advances "just one more level, Mom!" is likewise propelled by an inner drive to conquer the computer game.

Most children enter kindergarten similarly driven—excited about learning to read and write, enthusiastic and eager to learn about the world around them. As children grow, this inborn desire to learn can continue like a raging river, a gentle stream, or a tiny trickle. Sometimes it simply disappears into the mud. But you needn't sit back and watch your child's enthusiasm for learning vanish. You *can* have a child who looks forward to a history project or a chemistry experiment with the same thrill of anticipation she feels before the latest Disney movie or her league championship basketball game.

WHY SELF-MOTIVATION IS BETTER

Learning is higher in quality when children enjoy it. University of Rochester psychologist Richard Ryan and his colleagues showed this advantage of self-motivation in a study of ninety-two college students. They asked them to read either a passage on a new blood analysis technique or one about how Rudyard Kipling's writing derived from his own experiences. Next they assessed the students' interest in and enjoyment of their passage. A few minutes later, Ryan had the students write on a blank sheet everything they remembered from the reading. (He hadn't told the students they would be tested.) The greater the students' interest and enjoyment in reading the material, Ryan found, the more concepts they recalled from the passage, and the better they understood them.[3] A follow-up study showed that students' interest in material also helped them remember it over the long term.[4] These studies demonstrated that self-motivated students learn more, understand it better, and remember it longer than other students.

Another psychologist tested several hundred students, ages nine to thirteen, in one private and two public schools. Adele Eskeles Gottfried, a psychologist at California State University, Northridge, found that the more kids enjoyed academics generally, the higher were their standardized test scores and grades in reading, social studies, and science.[5] She also found that the more kids enjoyed schoolwork, the less anxious they were about it.

Other studies have shown that high-achieving students love learning more than other students[6] and that self-motivated students are more likely to take on academic work that is difficult.[7] They also perform complex tasks, which involve reasoning, inferring, and understanding, more competently than other students.[8]

UC Berkeley psychologist Marty Covington, who studied the academic motivation of 2,500 introductory psychology students, described his self-motivated students this way: "[They] feel poised and ready to learn and they seek knowledge above and beyond what's required. . . . They discover knowledge actively rather than acquiring it passively."

"They wonder more than they worry, and they even say that learning gives them intense and uplifting feelings," adds Covington. Several intrinsically motivated students told him that learning even helped them make better life choices and increased their compassion, patience, and personal courage.[9]

FLOW: LOVING LEARNING AT ITS MOST INTENSE

Learning can be so intense and enjoyable that it hurtles a student into a state that University of Chicago psychologist Mihaly Csikszentmihalyi calls "flow." Flow is a feeling of passionate focus, a pleasurable time when work and play merge, when you concentrate deeply to overcome complex challenges. "I no longer notice my fingers, the score, the keys, the room," said a pianist describing his flow state to Csikszentmihalyi. "Only my emotions exist and they come through my fingers."[10]

Most people "remember a time, no matter how brief, when they were swept along by a sense of effortless control, clarity, and concentration on an enjoyable challenge," explains Csikszentmihalyi. You can lose yourself to flow during a deep conversation or a game of chess, or while reading a riveting novel. Researchers have also observed flow in Web surfers who lose track of time while navigating through cyberspace.[11] A student in flow is so involved with her work that she isn't aware of what is going on around her or that she's hungry or tired.

Flow doesn't occur often for most people, but it's so intense and pleasurable that one dose is extremely powerful. Be on the lookout for flow states in your child, because it's a sure sign of intellectual enjoyment you can encourage.

More frequently you are likely to notice your child's self-motivation in a milder form. Perhaps he'll dig into his math homework and feel a solid sense of self-satisfaction when he's done. Maybe your daughter will look forward excitedly to school because she'll have an art lesson with colored pencils, or she's eager to write in her journal, or enthusiastic about the new reading book. Maybe your child is the kind who simply likes "learning new things," or maybe she's the kind who gobbles up any book about horses.

We see variation in our children because the desire to learn isn't uniform or consistent. It can be passionate or mild, steady or erratic, joyful or merely satisfying. But all forms of self-motivation have two qualities in common: like solar energy, they're self-renewing and they are inside your child, propelling him to learn.

As a parent, you can play an important role in fostering this inner desire to learn, sometimes even an intense involvement in learning. Let's plunge in now and look at some basic strategies for maximizing your child's love of learning, or reviving it if she's forgotten how much pleasure learning can bring.

Nurturing Your Child's Desire to Learn

Do you remember how determined your baby was to learn how to hold her bottle, open a cupboard, and walk? She was single-minded because infants and toddlers are wired to develop the knowledge and skills they need to negotiate the world effectively.

Likewise, children's enthusiasm flourishes when they realize that academics explains the world and equips them to deal with it successfully. Unfortunately, however, school learning seems irrelevant to most kids today. If you don't believe me, try this experiment. Ask your school-aged child these three questions about any assignment:

- Why do you think your teacher wanted you to do this?
- What will you learn from this assignment?
- Can you think of a way you'll use this knowledge or skill outside school?

Most likely your child will look at you with a puzzled expression. That's because most schools follow their own internal logic: students work, take tests, and are rewarded or punished for their performance. Rarely does anyone explain how (or whether) the curriculum will help students lead productive, compassionate, or otherwise successful lives. Most kids can't even explain what skill they're learning, let alone its usefulness outside the classroom. When asked why they're doing an assignment, they usually answer, "Because the teacher told us to."

Research has shown how teachers inadvertently foster this disconnection between learning and life. When Michigan State University psychologist Jere Brophy and his colleagues observed elementary school teachers introducing lessons, they found that teachers explained the purpose of only 1.5 percent of assignments.[12] During 317 introductions of new work, none of the teachers they observed said the assignment would help children develop useful or enjoyable skills. Quite the opposite: in 8 percent of the presentations the instructors explicitly said they didn't expect their students to like the work or do well on it! In only 3 percent of the lessons did the teacher show any enthusiasm or link the work to their students' lives or interests. In fact, several teachers made chilling comments like "This test is to see who the really smart

Of course, I'm not ruling out the possibility that some of your child's curriculum may *be* irrelevant. When I was in junior high school in the 1960s, we weren't allowed to do anything else in home economics until we learned how to make perfect baking powder biscuits. As a result, my class spent an entire semester making baking powder biscuits, a skill that seemed irrelevant to my life at the time. Despite this course, I love to cook now—but I still haven't grasped the singular importance of making a perfect baking powder biscuit.

ones are," or promoted anti-intellectualism with remarks like "Get your nose in the book—otherwise I'll give you a writing assignment."

But children are delighted when they discover that a concept learned in school explains an everyday experience. I remember my daughter, Meredith, enthusiastically explaining to me the pH of shampoo, and why we sometimes get a shock when we turn on the lights in dry weather.

BREATHE LIFE INTO SCHOOL LEARNING BY CONNECTING IT TO THE REAL WORLD

You can nurture your child's desire to learn by helping him link book learning to the real world. The more kids see such connections, the more meaningful their schoolwork will be, and the stronger will be their interest and pleasure in learning.

Of course, before you can help your child see the relevance of schoolwork to life, you have to know what your child is studying. Some kids, especially younger ones, will tell you what they're studying. If, however, you ask your child what she is learning in school and she doesn't answer, ask her to show you her math homework or where she is in her social studies text. Don't hesitate to ask her teacher what the class will cover in a particular month, or for a general sketch of this year's topics. You needn't know every little detail, just enough to help you make the school curriculum meaningful to your child.

Once you know what your child is studying, you can help her connect it to everyday experiences. Here are some ways to do that:

Connect Science Learning to the Natural World

- If your second-grader is studying weather, ask him whether you should take your umbrella when you go out on a dark cloudy day, and why dark clouds predict precipitation. Ask him to predict whether it will snow during the night by tracking the temperature on the outside thermometer over the course of the evening.
- If your daughter is studying the earth and the solar system, watch a sunset together. Ask her where the sun is going. If you call from a trip in another time zone, ask her why it's earlier where you are. Or ask why it's already dark where Grandma lives, but still daylight at home.

Link Social Studies or History to Current Events

- If your son is studying the westward movement of European Americans, tell him about a local Native American tribe's request for gambling rights on their land.
- When your daughter is studying municipal government, show her a newspaper article on the budget cutbacks causing a reduction in local library hours or the elimination of the bus route she takes to her piano lesson.

Connect Literature to Real-Life Experiences and Dilemmas

- William Shakespeare's *Romeo and Juliet*, the 1996 movie with Claire Danes and Leonardo DiCaprio, piqued teenagers' interest in Shakespeare by portraying the tragedy as a conflict between youth gangs.

You can make similar connections between the books your child is studying and his own experience, or a news event.

- If you don't have time to read the book, rent and watch the movie together after he's read the book.
- Or simply ask your child to tell you the story he's reading in school, and start a conversation on its relevance to your own or his experiences, to history or to current events: "Does that remind you of the time in kindergarten when you thought Jason wasn't going to be your friend anymore?" "That's how I felt when your grandfather died."

Point Out Math Applications in Daily Life

- If your daughter is having difficulty getting excited about her measurement unit in math, take her to her aunt's architecture office and ask her aunt to show her how important measuring is to her work.
- Show a fifth- or sixth-grader how proportions are used to compute baseball batting averages, how you have to add and divide fractions to double or halve a recipe, or how to use the math she's learning at school to calculate the increased value of the bonds you bought for her college fund.
- If you go to Canada or Mexico on vacation, involve your child in figuring out currency exchanges.

Make Connections That Are Meaningful for a Child

Make sure you connect schoolwork to your child's immediate or not-too-far-off experiences. "You need to learn how to add and subtract to balance your checkbook" won't mean much to a second-grader. And your eleven-year-old won't get excited about learning about the human circulatory system because "someday she may want to be a doctor."

Stay away, too, from general cheerleading like "You'll need to know this when you're a grown-up" or "I know you don't see now why you should learn this, but I know you'll be glad you did." Such well-meaning but abstract statements are more likely to elicit groans than pique interest.

EXPAND SCHOOL LEARNING

Another way to bring school learning alive is to broaden your child's experience, by taking her to places like museums, aquariums, farms, and historic sites. (Virtual visits to a Web site count too.)

Here are a few examples of ways to infuse your child's school curriculum with the color and fullness of reality:

- If your daughter is studying a local Native American group, take her to a museum or mission.
- If she is studying state government and you don't live too far from the capital, take her to a senate debate, or help her find on the Web some bills on a subject that interests her.
- If your son is studying marine life, take him to the beach to explore the tide pools, or to an aquarium.

If you can't think of an enrichment activity, ask your child's teacher or a librarian for a suggestion.

Everyday experience enhances school learning too. You may not

The historian Doris Kearns Goodwin traces her interest in Franklin and Eleanor Roosevelt, subjects of her 1994 biography, to the third grade, when she was assigned an oral report on FDR and her parents took her to visit Hyde Park.[13]

realize it, but those trips to the park, to a downtown with skyscrapers, and to Grandma's house, and the pet turtle or fishbowl your child has in his room all help him relate to what he reads and learns.

Broaden the scope of topics that your child is studying in school and bring them into your family life.

- If your daughter is learning about the Westward Movement, get an "Oregon Trail" game for her to play on her computer.
- When your son is doing a science unit on the desert, help him check out colorful and informative books on desert animals at the library. Read him one of the books at bedtime.
- If your daughter is learning about poetry, write a poem together, read poetry together from a book, or write out her favorite song and discuss its poetic features.
- Suggest your son ask questions about the historic event he is studying in school of a grandparent or neighbor who remembers it.

Don't rule out the possibility that your child is already interested and even passionate about a school subject. Sometimes it's obvious, as when your son blabs on and on about the Egyptian-style mural he's drawing for a social studies unit. Sometimes the teacher will tell you which subjects rouse the most enthusiasm in your child.

But frequently you need to do a little investigation. First, ask your child what subject she likes at school, or what she's learning that's interesting. If she replies, "Nothing" (as many children will), it's time to put on your Sherlock Holmes (or Nancy Drew) hat:

- What subjects does she mention at home? What topics does she ask questions about?
- Which homework assignments does she always do first? Which ones does she show you?
- What books does she choose at the library?

Try expanding first on a subject that already grabs your child's interests. With the pilot light already on, you'll be sure to get an enthusiastic response.

While it's good to make school curricula relevant for your child, you don't always have to start with the topics your child is learning in school. You can also help your child maintain his zest for learning by developing his own intellectual interests—and hope that a good teacher down the road will notice that spark and fan the flames.

ENCOURAGE YOUR CHILD'S INTERESTS AND PASSIONS OUTSIDE OF SCHOOL

Columnist Thomas Friedman, who spent many years as the *New York Times* Jerusalem correspondent, realized that the politics and people of the Middle East were his passion when his parents took him to Israel during his Christmas vacation at age fifteen. "I don't know if it was just the shock of the new, or a fascination waiting to be discovered, but something about Israel and the Middle East grabbed me in both heart and mind," he writes in *From Beirut to Jerusalem*.[14] "I was totally taken with the place, its peoples and its conflicts. Since that moment, I have never really been interested in anything else." (Friedman's interests, as readers of his column know, have since broadened.)

Similarly, Nel Noddings, a former professor of education at Stanford, traces her daughter's passion for geology to visits she and her husband organized for their children to the Museum of Natural History. "We couldn't get her away from the exhibit on gems, rocks, and the earth," Noddings remembers. The daughter is now a petroleum engineer.

Every child has interests and passions. They are either as conspicuous as Mount Rainier or lurking somewhere below ground, waiting to be unearthed. Your child may have a consuming passion for computers, or only a slim interest in recycling. Whatever the starting point, encouraging your child to develop intellectual passions is as important as making school curricula relevant. The more you encourage your child's hobbies, the more likely he'll develop his own intellectual interests—in bugs, story writing, chemistry, or music—and the more passion he will bring to related academics.

Nurturing your child's interests outside school is particularly important because, ironically, conditions at home are often more conducive to fostering passions than is the school environment. That's because at home your child is free to do what she likes. In school, kids typically have few choices; they're usually told what to learn, and how and when to learn it. Furthermore, at school kids are frequently evaluated and judged, which you needn't do at home. (I'll explain the chilling effect of evaluation by grades and tests in chapter 9.) Although some teachers are terrific at making subject matter interesting to their students, they are, unfortunately, in the minority.

Nel Noddings, who raised ten children, took to its extreme the principle of home as a place to nourish interests. She used to let her children stay home to finish a painting, clean the aquarium, or cook a Chinese dinner—as long as their absence didn't inconvenience a lab partner or oblige a teacher to give a makeup test. "I was afraid if they went to school too much they'd lose their intellectual interests entirely," remembers Noddings. "That was one reason I didn't force them. School can often be very boring."[15]

Enrich Your Child's Palette of Experiences

The best way to encourage interests is through direct experience. A child has to work or play on a computer to develop an interest in programming, and has to hear music to realize she wants to play a certain musical instrument, as concert cellist Jacqueline DuPre did after listening to a radio concert at the age of four:

One day Jackie was in the kitchen at home with Mum, who was ironing. The wireless was on and *Children's Hour* was presenting a program about the instruments of the orchestra. Mum was moving the iron in time to the music and Jackie was swaying from side to side in time with Mum's strokes. The flute, oboe and clarinet all had their turn, followed by the violins. As the sound of a cello filled the room, Jackie became completely still and attentive. She listened transfixed until the end, leapt up, clutched Mum's leg and said, "Mummy I want to make *that* sound."[16]

A rich array of experiences (which, we'll see in chapter 2, also promote reading comprehension) will help your child find passionate interests by giving her a wide range of choices. A visit to the seashore, a desert, or a fossil site may do the trick, or trips to museum exhibits, concerts, and plays. There's a lot to learn in your community. Even taking your child on a bus, to your work, or to the local farmer's market broadens her knowledge of the world and nurtures her curiosity. Although direct experience is usually better, books, movies, and the Internet will also broaden your child's horizons by taking him places that otherwise can't be visited—the Australian outback, medieval France, or the moon.

You can increase the chances that a new experience will stoke your child's intellectual fires by "embroidering" on or expanding it. For example,

- Get a star chart before a camping trip and try to find some of the constellations in the sky.
- Suggest your child choose an animal to study before or after you visit an aquarium or zoo. Get coloring books, storybooks, or use the Internet to investigate the animal.
- Take hikes led by naturalists or park rangers.
- Find out some interesting facts about the life of a composer or an artist before you go to a concert or museum.

- Look up Thailand on a map and read about it in an encyclopedia before eating at a Thai restaurant.

- Visit ethnic neighborhoods in large cities. Eat there, look at products in stores, and discuss how they're similar or different to those you're familiar with, and why.

- If you visit Mexico or Canada or another foreign country, or if you live in a city with large ethnic populations, point out simple words in another language like *arrêt* on stop signs or *panadería* on a bakery sign.

- Go to festivals celebrating holidays that are related (or not) to your child's own cultural background. Before or afterwards, read about the origins and meaning of the event.

- You don't even need to leave the comfort of your home. You can watch and talk about educational TV programs, or after watching a baseball game on TV, read the sports page together and talk about how an article is written or what it says about the Giants or the Phillies.

Fan the Flames

When your child has a passion (assuming it's safe and legal), fan the flames. One mother I know noticed that her five-year-old son liked to collect rocks. She took him to the Museum of Natural History, helped him find library books about geology, visited the nearby American Gemological Institute, and even planned a family vacation to Colorado, where rocks abound.

- If your daughter likes animals, join the zoo, subscribe to a natural science magazine, show her articles about animals in the newspaper, and help her find library books and videos on zoology.

- If she's interested in hair, clothes, and makeup, take her to a museum with a costume collection like the Smithsonian's, help her examine and

investigate the chemicals in makeup. Slip a book about medieval cloth-
ing onto the coffee table. Stimulate her creativity in design by getting
her a sketchbook or offering her art lessons.

- If your son likes computers, take him to a computer exposition when it
  comes to your city, subscribe to a computer magazine, and help him
  find a club or scout troop that takes apart and rebuilds computers.
- If your daughter loves soccer, show her articles in the sports section
  about the national women's team. You can also expand her interests
  by telling her about efforts to stop child labor in manufacturing soccer
  balls, or pointing out the words in other languages you hear at an
  international soccer match.

Don't be surprised if your child's interests change as he grows.
Richard Cohen, a former UES teacher, says his son's passions in elementary school were birds, rocks, and cooking. Now a teenager, his
son likes baseball, fantasy books like Tolkien's, and computers. "Don't
expect your child to develop a calling at age three," warns Cohen.[17]

On the other hand, early interests may evolve, as they did with my
son Zach. An ardent sports card collector and trader as a child, he has
always been interested in business. But now, as a college student, he
collects and trades shares in the stock market rather than baseball
cards.

LET YOUR CHILD BE LOPSIDED

It may seem paradoxical, but an important way to nurture your
child's passions is to allow him not to be interested in everything. In
America we admire the kid who's "best all-around," but in the long
run a slightly "lopsided" kid usually loves learning more.

"It isn't reasonable to suppose everyone has an intrinsic interest in
math any more than that everyone has an intrinsic interest in art,
drama or architecture," explains Nel Noddings, who taught high school
math before joining the faculty at Stanford. "When we think about all

the subjects kids are taught, then do we say 'You're going to have an interest in all those things'? Why would you? We often push on kids, we expect them to do their best on everything. No, we ought to say, 'Do an adequate job on the things you have to do, but do a superb job in the things that really interest you.'"[18]

Recognizing your child's passions may encourage him to work harder on his less favorite subjects, adds Noddings, because kids respond to adults who understand and approve of their interests. If your child loves drama or sports, letting him know that's fine with you may, ironically, motivate him to work on science and math, his less-favorite subjects, since he'll feel he's freely choosing to do so. (I'll explain more about the positive influence of "freely choosing" in chapters 5 and 6.)

ROLE-MODEL ENTHUSIASM FOR LEARNING

My friend Debbie has fond childhood memories of jumping up from the dinner table to find the dictionary or an encyclopedia volume to answer questions and settle family debates. Debbie's parents taught her the joy of learning by modeling their own. Role-modeling your enthusiasm in the same way will help create a culture of learning in your family. If you don't know the answer to a question your child asks, help her find it. Search the World Wide Web, visit the library, or call a friend who might know. In addition to modeling curiosity and pleasure in seeking knowledge, you'll teach your child valuable strategies for finding information.

I know your time is limited—mine is too. But when you can, pursue your own intellectual interests and hobbies. Whether your passion is jazz, photography, reading, antique trolley cars, Civil War memorabilia, or international politics, introduce your child to it. Take your daughter with you to a concert, a political meeting, or to work. Share with your son the fun you're having and what you're learning in a gardening or computer class.

Talk about your own passions at home while you do the dishes with your child, or while riding in the car or standing in line at the bank. Mention what interests you in movies, plays, or television shows you've watched together. Share something you learned watching the History Channel or in a magazine or newspaper. "It says here that the loss of the Mars Polar Lander is making NASA change its strategy for exploring Mars," you might say. Or "Did you know the government is trying to make gun makers manufacture guns that will be safer? Does that make sense to you?"

If you visit a museum, science exhibit, or zoo, don't walk around passively. Show (or pique) your curiosity by reading pamphlets and signs that explain the exhibits. If your child isn't interested, don't read him every single bit of information; instead, pick out facts or explanations likely to intrigue him, given his age:

- "It says here that there are only eleven white alligators in the entire world."
- "Did you know that the Impressionists preferred painting out of doors, in natural light? That must be why they use these bright colors."

Show your child *you* enjoy learning about what you see. If you don't enjoy it, get some background information to perk up your own interest before you go next time. Or go only to places you know you'll enjoy.

Refrain from modeling negative perspectives on learning. When discussing schoolwork, suppress negative comments that may spring to mind, like "Who ever said school should be fun?" or "Math is boring. You just have to slog through it and not take any more than you have to," or "I know you hate history, honey. I don't blame you. You won't remember any of it anyway."

Do show that you understand how your child feels. But then try to help her find a silver lining. "Didn't you say you get to choose any city you want to study for your social studies project? Maybe you could choose one you'd like to visit." "I know you don't like writing a lot of book reports, but look at the great books you're reading."

Warning: It's Always a Mixed Bag

While you strive to promote your child's enthusiasm for learning, keep in mind that love of learning rarely exists in a pure state. External incentives for academic work—such as grades, or parents' praise— nearly always exist side by side with self-motivation.

Isn't your own motivation nearly always mixed? For example, you may enjoy playing tennis or baseball, but also find it a good way to make business contacts. Or think about a college professor who is deeply interested in ancient Greek history or molecular physics. She is also kept going by her colleagues' praise for her scholarly contributions, psychologist Marty Covington points out—not to mention the salary increases pegged to the number of books and articles she publishes.[19]

Furthermore, it's common to drift in and out of "wanting to learn" during any project. While writing this book, for example, there were times when I purred along pleasantly, the words simply flowing through my fingers onto the keyboard, like Csikszentmihalyi's pianist, unaware of the passing of time and of any commotion in the house. But just as often, I had to make deals with myself: "If you keep working until 4:30, you can have a chocolate chip cookie." Kids are the same; they may be highly self-motivated, but still need some rewards, grades, or other external prods to keep going. You can, however, minimize the need for those nudges. Let's look now at how you can maximize your child's love of learning by taking advantage of his natural drive to learn through play.

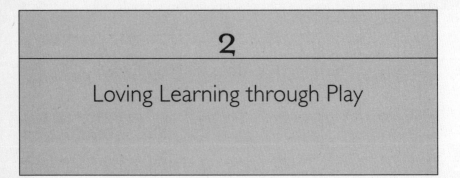

2

Loving Learning through Play

When my son Jeff was four, I walked into his preschool classroom at UES one day to find him and his best friend playing post office.[1] Their teacher had given them paper, pencils, envelopes, pretend money, and stamps. On the wall she'd tacked a poster; it had pockets labeled with each classmate's name where the two boys could "mail" their letters.

Jeff and Gabe couldn't read or write yet, but they were learning that people communicate by putting marks on paper. While their markings resembled Sumerian cuneiform more than English, the game strengthened the hand and eye coordination the boys would need for writing. Later in the year, when they'd learned the first letters of their names, their teacher suggested they mark *J* and *G* in the return address corner of the envelopes.

Jeff and Gabe's teacher had offered them a choice among several different activities, so they didn't feel pressured to play the post office game. Nor were they being graded. They played because they wanted to—because they enjoyed it. At the same time, the post office game was developing their language, thinking, and social abilities. The game looked simple, even frivolous, yet it was taking advantage of the boys' natural playfulness to launch their reading and writing skills.

Play is your child's first foray into loving learning. That's why many educators say, "Play is children's work."

How do we know that kids learn through play? Why didn't this UES teacher simply sit those four-year-olds down with a workbook and pencil and tell them to copy letters and numbers until they get it? She didn't because psychologists have found that young children learn best through play.

It Starts in Infancy

Swiss psychologist Jean Piaget researched this connection between play and learning by scrupulously observing his own children. When his son Laurent was ten months old, for example, Piaget noticed him dropping pieces of bread on the floor and watching carefully where they fell. This kind of behavior may sound familiar. Remember when your baby kept throwing his bottle or his teddy bear out of the crib, and you kept picking them up and telling him, "No, no, don't throw!" What may have seemed like stubbornness was really your baby's serious scientific study of the laws of gravity. "Do objects always fall down?" he was wondering (if not exactly in these words). "Or do they sometimes float up? Or do bottles fall down, and teddy bears float up?" Through play, your baby was learning about the natural world.

Piaget noticed another kind of play a year later. When his son was a year and a half and saw a cat on the garden wall, he began carrying a seashell around in a box, saying, "Meow, meow!"[2] Piaget explained that this game of pretending that the seashell was a cat showed that Laurent understood that one thing could stand for another.

In fact, all kids at about eighteen months to two years old seem compelled to practice their budding ability to think symbolically. That's why they pretend to drink out of an empty cup, ride a broomstick like a horse, or point at a bus or a computer screen, asking over and over, "What's that?" This symbolic understanding they are developing is extremely important, because it's a prerequisite for learning to read, write, and do math.

LEARNING THROUGH PLAY CONTINUES
THROUGH THE PRESCHOOL YEARS

As they leave babyhood, children continue to seek knowledge actively and playfully. Watch your toddler do puzzles, draw pictures, or investigate the cat's reaction to pulling its tail. Her exploration may seem random or even devilish, but in fact she's learning about perspective, shapes and colors, and cause and effect, and she's acquiring a million other facts and concepts she needs to be effective in the world.

This kind of hands-on learning is more productive for preschoolers than paper and pencil work, and it keeps alive children's internal motivation to learn. As psychologist Jerome Bruner said, "I have . . . studied hundreds of hours of play behavior. I have never, in all that time, seen a child glaze over or drop out or otherwise turn off while engaged in play. I wish I could say the same for the children I have observed in classrooms and even in one-to-one tutorials."[3]

So the next time your toddler tosses a toy out the car window or pours his milk on the table to see which way it flows, you may feel less exasperated. Now you know that kids gain from these playful explorations the intuitive understandings they'll need to grasp formal scientific concepts later in school. Perhaps dropping Styrofoam peanuts into the tub to see if they float, for example, will pay off when your child's fifth- or sixth-grade teacher explains relative density.

Children's spontaneous investigation and manipulation of the world are so universal that Piaget and other psychologists after him concluded that kids are wired to learn: they are naturally driven to practice skills, adding a layer of competence or understanding with each repetition. After perfecting one skill, they stretch themselves by moving on to a game that's a little different or more complicated.

This natural drive for understanding and skill development explains even why your preschooler watches the same cartoon video over and over, and then suddenly loses interest. Young children have to listen many times to fully understand a simple plot and set of characters. But as soon as they master it, they lose interest, because they're no longer challenged and no longer learning by watching it.

THE VALUE OF PLAY DOESN'T END AT FIVE

Learning through play isn't just for preschoolers. It continues throughout school, and indeed throughout life. When seven-year-olds play board games they sharpen their social skills, learning to negotiate and to be a good sport. And depending on the game, they may also hone their thinking skills. Ten-year-olds develop planning and organizational abilities when they bake a cake or build a model airplane. Chess and bridge help teenagers think hypothetically and consider multiple variables simultaneously.

Adults learn through play too. When I have time, I read French novels for fun, but in the process I develop my French vocabulary. My father, in his eighties, takes courses at his local junior college in Spanish and law.

We call such learning "play" because it's undertaken for enjoyment rather than for a practical purpose or a reward. But adults still learn from these activities. In fact, some psychologists believe that adults who play often are more productive. The most creative adults, said the psychoanalyst Erik Erikson, are those with least separation in daily life between work and play.[4]

Promoting Your Preschool Child's
Playful Learning at Home

Most parents instinctively participate in playful learning with their infants. When your baby grabs your finger and plays mini-tug-of-war, you help him develop motor skills without even realizing it. When you play peek-a-boo, you're teaching him about the permanence of objects—that Mommy and Daddy exist, even when they are out of sight.

But there are also conscious steps you can take to link learning with enjoyment, capitalizing on your child's eagerness to learn through play. Here are some ways you can spark playful learning:

TIME AND PLACE

First and foremost, give your child lots of time for free play. And make sure she has a place: a playroom, a backyard, or a corner of the living room to play safely.

MATERIALS

Second, provide some props for your child's play. But don't put a lot of expensive "educational toys" on your credit card. Kids benefit more from active manipulation and exploration than from passive watching, so simple toys that demand imagination are better than flashy battery-powered cars or talking dolls, which limit what your child can do. Complicated toys that dictate a specific activity are fun at first, but children usually lose interest in them quickly because they don't allow them to experiment, explore, or create.

"The more the child can do with the toy, the more likely it is to be truly educational," says educator Janet Brown McCracken.[5] Flexible toys, like blocks, Legos, Lincoln logs, Ramagon, and Brio toys, allow kids to exercise their imaginations and to take satisfaction and pride in their creations.

Legos, for example, will allow your child to build almost anything she can imagine—just like computer scientists, who use Legos to create robotic prototypes. "Any brick can attach to any other brick," explained a Brandeis University researcher when asked why he likes to use the modular toys.[6]

Block play teaches children about shapes, colors, geometry, and gravity, and lets them practice planning and sharing. The flexibility of blocks allows them to adapt to children's ever-increasing skill levels. Two-year-olds can examine differently shaped and colored blocks, clap them together, and push them around on the floor. Three- and four-year-olds can build towers or dictate a story to you about the dragons that live in their block buildings. Five- and six-year-olds can build a house with a chimney and two dogs in the yard.

You can also give your child everyday objects—empty boxes, toilet paper, and paper towel rolls—to stimulate her experimentation and creativity. Kids also like to cut and paste fabric pieces, ribbons, and magazines; inexpensive art materials, like markers, crayons, paint, and beads, are fun too.

Make sure to give your child some "representational" toys, like cars, puppets, stuffed animals, miniature dishes, and furniture, to stimulate her pretend play. Toy cars and trucks will help your child develop notions of distance and space. Small toys, like farm animals, shells, and marbles, will give him a chance to match, group, and compare, and to develop his language skills by making up stories. Musical instruments—harmonicas, triangles, plastic flutes, and drums (if you can stand them)—will allow him to explore sounds and patterns.

Sand, mud, and water make good play materials too, because they give children firsthand experiences with different textures and substances. Enhance your child's learning in the bathtub or sandbox by giving her a measuring cup, objects that will sink or float, and buckets, shovels, or molds that will allow her to investigate by "playing around" with these solids and liquids.

LET YOUR CHILD BE IN CHARGE

Most children will play with simple toys without any help. Indeed, what's really remarkable is that, given a choice, they usually choose activities that are "just right," those that help them develop precisely the physical and intellectual skills they need at that time in their lives. That's why Jeff and Gabe chose the post office game rather than an activity that wouldn't teach them anything new or that was too difficult.

Although little kids tend to choose their activities wisely, you can support and stretch your child's play, as Jeff and Gabe's teacher did when she added new wrinkles to the post office game as the year progressed.

But be careful not to take over. Research has shown that when parents try to control their children's play, intervene to solve problems, or finish projects themselves, their children tend to become passive and end up learning less. For example, the Dutch psychologist P. Lütken-haus watched mothers playing with their three-year-olds. Kids whose mothers intruded, by pushing their hand in a direction or taking a toy from them, enjoyed the activity less and were more likely to stop playing than kids whose moms were less intrusive and simply responded to their requests for help.[7]

Here are some ways to nudge and guide your child's play without controlling it:

- Model behaviors: show your baby in his bath how to fill and pour water out of a cup.
- Provide props: give your galloping daughter a broomstick or a scarf for reins; give a carrot to your son, the bunny rabbit.
- Assist: hand your preschooler the puzzle pieces one by one.

- Play a role: place a call from mission control to invite your astronaut daughter to lunch.[8]

You can also get seriously involved in your child's pretend play, as this father did one day after work.

DAD: What are your dollies doing?

JANINE: They're having a tea party.

DAD: What kind of tea are they drinking?

JANINE: It's sweet.

DAD: Can I have some?

JANINE: Okay.

DAD: Yummy! This is delicious tea! What makes it so sweet?

JANINE: Sugar. Want more?

DAD: Yes, please. Are we at home or at a restaurant?

JANINE: It's a hotel.

DAD: Oh, of course. Where is the hotel?

JANINE: Pennsylvania.

DAD: If this is a hotel, don't I have to pay for my tea?

JANINE: Yes, that will be ten dollars.

DAD: Ten dollars is a little steep. Here's a nickel and a penny. That's six cents, because a nickel is the same as five cents. Now I think I'll go up to room 102 and take a nap.

Notice that Janine's father plays along with her scenario, embellishing it just a bit. Without shifting the theme of the play, he manages to introduce the social studies concept of "payment for goods and services," and even a little math.

Like Janine's father, let your child stay in charge. Don't tell her to build a tower of blocks, but if she decides to build one, challenge her to "build a tall one." If your son is a zookeeper, ask what animal you should be. When your preschooler gets stuck doing a puzzle, point out that the piece she is looking for is tall and skinny, or has red on it, but don't hand her the piece. If she is playing school, ask, "Do you want me to get out your brother's kindergarten school books?" Don't say, "I'll give you a math lesson."

Always give your child only the help he needs to finish a project on his own. Don't suggest changes or correct him unless he asks you to. If you do, you'll turn his play into work, dampening his desire to learn playfully.

Learning Basic Academic Skills through Play

Most of the play that children begin themselves helps them develop the motor skills and thinking that form a basis for later academic learning. But you can also lend that development a hand.

The best way to introduce your child to basic academic skills is through everyday chores and playful activities. Sprinkling a few "games" throughout your child's day will also foster the attitude that learning is fun.

PRESCHOOLERS

Most young children find drills and worksheets boring. They'll do them if you force them, or if it's the only way to get your praise, but they usually don't enjoy them. Games, on the other hand, can teach basic skills while promoting enthusiasm for learning.

Here are some examples of games for teaching basic skills to three- to seven-year-olds:

- Chutes and Ladders: When your four- or five-year-old rolls the dice and counts the same number of spaces on the board, he'll learn counting, one-to-one correspondence (one count for each space), and other basic number concepts.

- Card games like Go Fish, War, UNO, and Oh No! 99 teach counting and the concept of matching and mismatching, or same and different.
- When playing checkers, ask your child how many checkers he has and how many you have. Then ask, "Who has more?"
- Teach your child the alphabet song.

SCHOOL-AGE CHILDREN

You can continue to promote basic skills learning through play throughout elementary school. Many computer games are fun and educational. (But don't take "educational" advertising claims at face value.) Here are examples of some games and activities that build vocabulary, writing, and math skills:

- Read a play together. You can read the male parts while your child takes the female parts (or vice versa).
- Build problem-solving skills by playing Twenty Questions on long car trips. (One person thinks of a person or thing, and the other has twenty yes or no questions to figure it out.)
- Choose a "word of the day" and put it into silly (but meaningful) sentences.
- Explain about angles and measurement while building a bookcase or doghouse together.

BE DISCRIMINATING AND DON'T BE AFRAID TO SAY NO

Not all play produces learning. Children enjoy plenty of activities that don't strengthen any skills. Watching TV, for example, can be fun, and although some TV shows may expand the mind, most simply numb the brain and encourage children to be couch potatoes interested mainly in toys and cereal. Some computer games help children develop basic technology literacy, as well as spatial and other skills,[9] but others are so repetitive they simply hypnotize. Some kids become so fixated on video games that they have little time for anything else. Don't hesitate to "just say no" to video games or restrict your child to a set number of hours a week. My sister-in-law Susie has banned all computer games for her two sons on weekdays, and allots them only a few hours on weekends. I think that's a sound policy.

Play can even be harmful. Games can promote antagonism and conflict, not friendliness or cooperation. For example, research suggests that endless hours at computer games with violent themes desensitize children to feelings like fear and horror, and can promote aggressive, even violent behavior.[10] Clearly, your guidance is important, even in play.

But when learning and play *do* come together, it's a dynamite mix, one well worth nurturing.

Learning Social Skills through Play

Increasing numbers of elementary schools are reducing and even eliminating recess time. This is a shame, because children learn invaluable skills by playing with other children.

In addition to building healthy bodies, group play develops crucial social as well as thinking skills. Just as young monkeys, according to

Some Americans feel that learning is always hard work and should *never* be fun. "I had to do it when I was a kid," they say, "and if I had to suffer, so will you." "This idea may be rooted in our Puritan forebears, to whom fun always meant sin," said the psychoanalyst Erik Erikson, author of the landmark book *Childhood and Society*. Or perhaps the notion derives from the Quakers, who thought we should "gather the flowers of pleasure in the fields of duty"—that is, seek pleasure only in work.[11]

zoologists, develop intelligence and problem-solving abilities through huge amounts of playtime, group recreation helps kids learn to share, empathize, help, and get along with others, as well as develop intimate friendships. Children learn important social problem-solving skills from negotiating conflicts in such games as cards, hopscotch, or touch football. Play also gives kids practice in cooperation, leading and following, communicating their ideas and listening to those of others. Hearing peers reason at a slightly higher level develops children's thinking abilities.

So by the time he's three, if your child isn't in preschool and has no neighborhood playmates, siblings, or cousins who live nearby, start a play group, or find some other way for him to play regularly with other kids his age. Give them toys that promote cooperative interaction—balls, a telephone, or a wagon for little ones, and card and board games as they grow older.

Learning about Emotions through Play

Four-year-old Seth watched his parents argue loudly. Later in his room, he spoke for his two favorite stuffed animals, mimicking his angry parents. "I'm tired of having to work all day then come home to dirty dishes," said the bunny rabbit. "Well, if you would ask me instead of accusing me, you might get somewhere!" replied the teddy bear. Then Seth had them hug each other and say, "We won't fight anymore!"[12]

Just as it helped Seth soothe his anxieties after seeing his parents fight, pretend play helps kids work out all sorts of emotional puzzles. With the figurative toys you've gathered—such as dolls, furniture, and farm animals—your child can play dramatically, experimenting with tenderness by caressing a doll, or with remorse when a teddy bear apologizes for not cleaning up his toys. Don't worry or interfere if you overhear your child playing out a fantastic scenario. She's only exercising her imagination and developing the emotional understanding she'll need to cope with challenging situations as she grows.[13]

Developing Dispositions for Learning

Katie, age four, stacks rectangular blocks carefully on end, trying to build a tower. But every time she places the third block on top of the other two, the tower tumbles to the floor. After a few failures, she lays the first block flat on the rug, the second block lengthwise on top of it, and perches the third on the top. This structure holds for a few seconds, then collapses. Katie is encouraged, but knows she hasn't quite figured out the secret of tower construction. After a little more experimenting with blocks in different positions, she finally builds a tower that stays up until her two-year-old brother drives a truck through it.

Katie is learning a lesson that will serve her well in school and in life—that persistence pays off. She's discovering that she can overcome frustration and setbacks, and that if she keeps trying different strategies, the wonderful feeling of satisfaction that comes with achieving a challenging goal will be hers.

Play is the perfect medium for encouraging these all-important habits of exploration, perseverance, and risk taking, because it has wide boundaries and there's no punishment for failing to reach a goal. Free from worry about their performance, children can try anything, experiment, and explore. This early play can become a model for the way they think and solve intellectual problems as adults. As Jerome Bruner explained it, "Playful, negotiatory, flexible, mindful interaction early on may become a model later for what you do when you encounter problems. Having played around in fact, and with good effect, you may now feel encouraged to play around in your own head."[14]

Beware of the Enemies of Play

When the writer Letty Cottin Pogrebin was nine years old, she decided to publish a magazine. Working in her bedroom, she wrote articles,

Child's play can lay the foundation for creative contributions in adulthood. When the neurologist Oliver Sacks was a boy, he played with enough potassium cyanide in his homemade chemistry lab to blow up greater London. Working with these dangerous chemicals brought him, he says, "respect and responsibility, as well as providing intellectual delight and fun."[15]

Similarly, when the Nobel laureate scientist Linus Pauling was eleven, he used copper sulphate and other "interesting" chemicals to carry out "delightful and spontaneous" experiments, which "set the stage for his entire creative life," says Sacks. "Would Pauling have become Pauling," he asks, "without this early play?"[16]

ads, cartoons, and even letters to the editor. She printed thirty copies of her four-page publication on a hectograph (a primitive printing press) and distributed it monthly to friends and family. "I charged three cents a copy because that's what newspapers cost in New York in those days, and I mailed each copy with a three-cent stamp, and never understood why the magazine didn't make a profit," she laughs.[17]

How many kids today have enough free time to play around with publishing a magazine? So many of our children instead are overstructured: Tuesday they have violin lessons, and Wednesday swimming practice. If it's Thursday, it must be karate and math tutoring. Weekends are devoted to soccer and scouts. Summer camp has to include science or computer lessons to impress college admissions officers. When all this activity is added to their homework, many children never have a chance to mess around with a chemistry set, giggle over a book of riddles, or collect bugs in the backyard. What child these days has enough free time to launch a lawn weeding business or build a clubhouse? Every minute is filled with expectations to become expert, compete, or perform.

If children don't have time of their own, they won't be able to explore their own interests and reap all the other benefits of play.

Unfortunately, several trends are conspiring to eliminate play from our children's lives. The culprits are well known: TV expands into the nooks and crannies of free time. Single and two-parent working families have frenzied schedules. Even the commercialization of national holidays tends to replace family games and celebrations with shopping and television.

Don't feel guilty for letting your kids watch some TV, especially when you're frazzled and desperately need some peace and quiet. But that's different from making TV the "default" activity to which your child gravitates whenever there's "nothing else to do." Try limiting her to a few shows, and keep a box of paints, paper, glue, and other materials handy to bring out when she's bored.

Tufts University psychologist David Elkind says we are eliminating playtime because we have redefined children from innocent to competent. We are doing so, he believes, because we can't protect them from the mountain of adult information and the many new risks they confront. We want to believe they can cope with these dangers themselves. "No longer is play seen as imaginative and preparatory, but rather it is now regarded as didactic and competitive," says Elkind.[18]

Surely the recent trend toward parents spending thousands of dollars for coaching and training their children to excel in one sport rather than to enjoy many of them is one sign of this loss of innocence.

Another sign that our children are not playing enough comes from engineering professors who say their students haven't fooled around with Erector sets or taken apart radios, bicycles, and telephones the way they used to. Henry Petroski, chair of Duke University's department of civil and environmental engineering, says that, as a result, many students have trouble imagining practical applications of engineering theory. A recent informal study of eminent engineers, he adds, found that as children they had played a lot with construction toys and at taking apart and reassembling kitchen appliances, bicycles, and cars.[19] To

The educational role of play for children is not a new idea. Two millennia ago, Socrates advised his fellow Greeks in Plato's *Republic* to "let early education be a sort of amusement; you will then be better able to find out the [child's] natural bent ... knowledge which is acquired under compulsion has no hold on the mind."[20]

close this gap, Stanford University has courses in which engineering students who missed this experience when they were younger take apart and reassemble a Corvette, a Pinto transmission, and a cordless drill.

Play and high-quality learning are inextricably linked. So don't crowd your child's schedule to the point of exhaustion. And if he's in an after-school program, make sure it has free play times. Don't worry if your child is not always busy. Allow her time to explore—and to dream. The more your child learns through play and the more her intellectual life is infused with fun, the more her natural motivation to learn will flourish, and the more likely she'll love learning her whole life long.

Now that you've laid the foundation with plenty of play, let's turn to the three components of loving learning: competence, autonomy, and relationship.

3

Nothing Motivates Children More Than Competence

One Saturday morning when my daughter, Meredith, was six, I took her to our neighborhood park for her first tee-ball game. After striking out twice, she was so discouraged she wanted to go home. I tried to boost her spirits by praising her for trying, but she was unmoved. Since I wanted her to learn persistence, I insisted she stay a little while. Finally, on her third time at bat, Meredith connected. The ball dribbled into center field and she dashed gleefully to first base. The next batter sent her speeding around the bases to score a run. Suddenly my daughter was an eager participant, chattering with her teammates and pestering her coach with, "When do I go up again?" On her next at-bat she hit another single. By the end of the game Meredith was so enthusiastic she didn't want to go home!

Nothing motivates children more than a feeling of competence. In fact, feelings of competence motivate us all. When I finally figured out how to record TV movies on the VCR while I wasn't home, I had such a feeling of achievement I taped a bunch of movies I didn't even care about.

Perhaps you remember a similar feeling of satisfaction after learning how to fix a leaky faucet or open an e-mail enclosure. Learning something new often feels so good we can't wait to do it again.

This same feeling of satisfaction and pleasure motivates small children to learn. That's why they insist on practicing newly developing skills, like turning doorknobs or taking off their shoes over and over again, oblivious to any nuisance or delay they're causing. Children's drive toward competence is so strong they sometimes persist even when the results are painful. Think, for example, of the one-year-old "punished" by repeated falls when she tries to walk. Just try and stop her from trying again!

Older children feel the same sense of satisfaction when they develop new skills. Your nine-year-old may enjoy eating the chocolate chip cookies she made, but the feeling of competence from producing a successful batch is equally rewarding.

Simply put, we all like activities that make us feel competent.

The motivating effect of feeling competent has tremendous significance for learning. Research has shown again and again that the more competent kids feel academically, the more interested they are in their schoolwork, and the harder they study. In other words, competence breeds self-motivation. The feeling of exuberance after even a single success in a difficult activity—from getting the first sound out of a clarinet to solving a complicated math problem—can keep a child working for a long time.

The power of feeling competent is a fairly recent discovery, launched in the 1950s, when psychologist Robert White took up where Piaget's observations of his infants (chapter 2) left off. In comparison to many other animals, White noticed, humans are born helpless and dependent. Our survival thus depends heavily on acquiring skills. Therefore, White explained, as a result of evolution a drive toward competence has earned a place in our internal hardwiring. Sustaining this drive is the feeling of pleasure, satisfaction, or pride that results from new accomplishments. Just as sexual pleasure ensures reproduction, the pleasure we feel from becoming competent keeps us striving for the competencies we need to survive. Like sex, competence is self-reinforcing: it feels good in and of itself.

Feelings of incompetence, on the other hand, are unpleasant and kill our motivation. We avoid activities that make us feel frustrated or inadequate. For example, since I have a bad memory for pop cultural facts, I've always hated Trivial Pursuit. Similar feelings of incompetence explain why I avoid chess and conversations about hard science.

Since competence is like an engine driving motivation to learn, the more you help your child develop academic competencies, the stronger will be his self-motivation—the more eagerly he'll study and the more willing he'll be to persist when the going gets tough. In this chapter I will show you how to promote feelings of competence in your child.

Challenge: The Key to Competence

Do people prefer easy tasks because they are sure to succeed? You might think so. But when there's no reward or punishment expected for success or failure, the opposite is usually true. Because success in easy work doesn't increase competence, it doesn't produce feelings of accomplishment, satisfaction, or pride. Our hardwiring to become competent makes us prefer "the stretch"— the challenge that is neither too hard nor too easy, but "just right" for increasing our competence.

Indeed, research shows that when given a free choice, kids select this optimum challenge, the task that lies one step beyond their current skill level. In one such study, for example, psychologist Ed Lonky and two colleagues tested ninety kids ages five through nine on three increasingly difficult activities, ranging from sorting blocks to solving a fairly complex puzzle. When they later allowed the kids to choose one of the three activities for ten minutes, *all* of them spent the most time working at the activity just beyond their current skill. They also rated that "one-step-ahead" activity the most interesting of the three.[1]

In other words, just as you might choose the ski run a bit higher than the one you just conquered, kids gravitate toward the activity that's neither too easy nor too hard, the "just-right" challenge that will boost their competence to the next level. That's why toddlers stop turning doorknobs for fun and move on to something that requires greater coordination, and why preschoolers get bored with simple puzzles and move on to harder ones. Success on tasks they've already mastered doesn't give them an exhilarating feeling of competence any more than doing a simple addition problem or boiling water would excite you (whereas learning to use a spreadsheet or cooking a gourmet meal might).

Researcher Susan Harter has documented the pleasure children get from this optimum challenge. Harter studied the smiles of fifth- and sixth-graders as they solved anagrams. The children whipped through the easy puzzles without much smiling. When working at the hardest ones, they barely smiled at all, and told the researchers they felt annoyed and frustrated. They smiled most, Harter found, when they solved anagrams that were neither too easy nor too hard for them. In other words, they found the most pleasure in the "just-right" challenge, the one they needed to increase their competence.[2]

So when you play catch with your daughter and she cries out, "Throw it harder this time!" or when you're quizzing your son on multiplication tables and he says, "Give me a really hard one," they are seeking the feeling of satisfaction and competence that the "just-right" challenge will give them.

This optimal challenge plays a part in the "flow" experience mentioned in chapter 1: research has shown that children are most likely to experience flow during academics when they have clear goals, receive immediate, specific feedback, and are working hard just at or slightly above their skill level.

Is Your Child Getting the "Just-Right" Challenge at School?

Although teachers ideally should give "just-right" work to each student, this isn't easy in a class of as many as thirty children. Teachers tend to aim toward the middle of the class, which sometimes means assigning work that is too difficult for some children and too easy for others. If your child isn't an eager learner, work that is not at the appropriate level of difficulty might be part of the problem.

It is not always easy to tell whether your child is facing just-right challenges at school, although you probably have some inkling. Here's how to test your hunch:

IS THE WORK TOO EASY?

Answers to the following questions will reveal whether your child's work is challenging enough to spur his enthusiasm:

- Does he call the work easy?
- Does she finish her homework quickly, with little effort?
- Does he get high grades on tests without much studying?
- Are the books she reads for pleasure more difficult than the books she's assigned to read at school?
- Does he consistently get perfect or close-to-perfect scores on assignments and tests?
- Does she fall apart when she encounters a little bit of difficulty? (This shows that she hasn't learned how to cope with the initial hurdles that always accompany challenging work—often a sign that she isn't getting enough of it.)

If the answer to even one or two of these questions is yes, your child's work may be too easy, and you need to share your observations with her teacher.

You should also explain to your child why challenging work is important, encouraging her to seek harder work so she can develop her skills. Brainstorm ways she can create more challenges for herself at school. Could she choose tougher topics for reports, take on the extra-credit brainteasers, or otherwise set higher standards? You might also suggest she try out for the citywide spelling contest, join the after-school geography club, or take a science class at the local museum during the summer.

Challenging work is particularly important for children who always do well in school. Success comes too easily to many high-achieving children, and some rarely face any difficulty. As a result, they don't learn how to cope with academic challenges, nor do they develop a strong sense of confidence in their ability to rise to the occasion.

IS THE WORK TOO HARD?

Clues that work is too hard are often subtle, as illustrated in the following exchange between a mom and her son:

MOM: Will you please get going on your homework? It's almost dinnertime.

RYAN *(sitting on his knees in the den, his hands on a joystick, his eyes on his video game)*: I will. I just want to finish this game.

(Twenty minutes pass.)

MOM: Aren't you finished with that game yet? Ryan, you haven't spent five minutes on homework, and you have a math test tomorrow.

RYAN *(sulkily walking toward his room)*: Okay, okay. Give me a break, willya?

(Mom looks into Ryan's room just before bedtime. She finds him lying on the floor trying to spin a basketball on his right index finger.)

MOM: This doesn't look like studying to me. Don't you have a math
   test tomorrow? Are you ready for it?

RYAN: As ready as I'm going to be.

MOM: What does that mean? Did you study for it?

RYAN: I'll study on the bus on the way to school tomorrow.

Most kids don't want to admit incompetence. Some, like Ryan, promise to work, then don't. Others go through the physical motions but their minds are elsewhere. Still others complain that an assignment is boring or stupid, or way too easy—when the real problem is that they don't know how to do it.

Occasionally children are all too happy to proclaim incompetence, declaring that their work is "too hard" or protesting, "I don't know how to do it." In this case you need to find out whether the work, in fact, is too hard, or whether she's just trying to get you off her back.

To cut through the subterfuge, have a discussion with your child. Let her know you love her, regardless of her achievement, grades, or competencies. Make sure you are not angry when you talk, and don't mention penalties or rewards. Your child needs to feel loved and respected to be able to share her feelings of inadequacy.

Begin with something like "You're such a great kid, Sam, but I'm worried about your schoolwork and want to know if there is anything I can do to help." Avoid accusing or threatening language, such as "I want to know why you refuse to put any effort into your schoolwork," or "If you don't start buckling down, you're going to be sorry."

Specific queries are better than general questions. Instead of "Do you understand what you are doing in science?" ask direct questions about particular work. "Do you know where you are supposed to get the information for your science report?" "Did you understand the plot of the book you have to write the report on?" "Do you know how to do these math problems?"

Sometimes children don't know why they're not trying. All they know is that they "don't feel like it." If your child is unable or unwilling to explain her lack of motivation, ask her to show you her assignments.

First, ask her what she's supposed to do. Sometimes children have the skills they need, but they aren't clear about the assignment.

If she understands the assignment but claims she "can't do it," try to get her started so you can see exactly what she can and can't do. Ask specific questions: "What do you need to do first?" "What part of the problem seems confusing?" If she's supposed to read something, have her read several paragraphs out loud. Then ask her a few questions to see if she understands it.

Sometimes children need only a little encouragement to get them going. But you may find that your child really doesn't have the skills or understanding he needs to finish his work. Then you need to make a plan with him to acquire them, and probably to have a conversation with his teacher.

Although school is the place we think most learning takes place, the truth is that kids' informal learning at home and in the community contributes tremendously to their academic competence. You can help build your child's intellectual skills starting at birth and continuing throughout the school years. I'm not suggesting you take a leave of absence from work to spend more time teaching your child. We send our children to school to learn, and for the most part, teaching is the teacher's responsibility, not yours. But I am suggesting that you bring activities into your family's everyday life to promote your child's competencies in the three Rs and beyond.

Preparing Your Toddler and Preschooler to Be Competent in School

We'll soon discuss strategies for helping your child develop the skills she needs to do her schoolwork. But first, see what you can do to make sure your child has the competencies she needs when she enters kindergarten.

BATHE YOUR CHILD IN LANGUAGE

Children's verbal skills are very important for learning to read and write. The larger your child's vocabulary when she starts kindergarten, for example, the better reader she'll be. But you needn't go out and buy vocabulary flash cards. Simply talk to your child.

Florida Atlantic University psychologist Erika Hoff-Ginsberg showed how conversations with parents build a child's vocabulary. She video-taped mothers while they dressed, fed, and played with their eighteen- to twenty-nine-month-old children, and analyzed the mother-child conversations. Few differences were found among the mothers while playing with their kids. But during dressing and eating, about half of the moms talked 25 percent more to their children, used a richer vocabulary, and asked more questions than the other half. For example, the more verbal moms used an average of 190 different words during breakfast, compared to 148 used by the others. The children of the more verbal mothers, Hoff-Ginsberg found, had larger vocabularies.[3]

I'm *not* suggesting you carry on a nonstop monologue like this one:

MOM: Now it's time to get dressed. What color T-shirt do you want to wear today? The blue? The yellow? Oh, look at these pretty flowers. Let's wear the shorts with the pretty flowers today. Oh look, these shorts have buttons on them instead of snaps!

Instead, make your conversation a two-way exchange, so your child not only hears new vocabulary and correct ways of speaking, but also practices her language skills.

MOM: What color T-shirt do you want to wear today? Blue or yellow?
JENNY: The yellow one.

MOM: You really like that yellow one, don't you? Is yellow your favorite color?

JENNY: No, I like the flowers.

MOM: What kind of flowers do you like?

JENNY: Yellow ones.

MOM: Can you think of any other flowers you like?

JENNY: The flowers on the walls in the bathroom.

MOM: Those are daisies. So shall we only buy you clothes with flowers on them from now on? Or do you want a little variety?

JENNY: What's "variety"?

MOM: Different colors and designs for different days—maybe yellow flowers today and blue balloons tomorrow.

JENNY: I don't want balloons.

MOM: Why don't you like balloons?

Note how Jenny's mom asks questions and builds on Jenny's comments, expanding her vocabulary naturally in a conversation.

Stories also teach verbal skills in a pleasurable way. Practice in listening to stories and telling them teaches children about the importance of paying attention to the sequencing of events, and of giving listeners all the details they need to know.

- Listen attentively and patiently to the stories your child tells you about her own experiences or what she's learned from movies or books. Encourage her to elaborate: "Tell me more. What happened after the dog jumped out of his bath?"
- Ask her to fill in missing information: "Which girl fell into the lake?"
- As your child grows, ask questions that provoke more than simple answers: "What does this photograph remind you of?" "How do you think the kitty feels now?"
- Point out words he hears but might not understand: "Did you know what the lady meant when she said you were mischievous?"

- Invite your toddler or preschooler to make up stories, and write them down while she tells them. Write exactly what your child says. That will show her how words on paper represent spoken words. Collect her stories in a folder or notebook. You'll be amazed at how much richer and more complicated they become over time.
- Teach your child songs, poems, rhymes, and wordplay games, like opposites ("What's the opposite of cold? Of big? Of yummy?").

PROMOTING READING SKILLS

One of the best predictors of how well children learn to read in school is how much they were read *to* before they began school. If you read to your child regularly, reading will be important and pleasurable to her, and her vocabulary will grow by leaps and bounds. She'll also learn "preliteracy" skills, like knowing that books are read left to right, that a story has a beginning, middle, and end, and that pictures tell you about the story.

So weave reading into your child's routine from babyhood onward: give her a book for the car seat, keep a few books among her toys, and visit bookstores for family recreation. There are even books you can buy for the bathtub! Bedtime reading creates a wonderful, intimate time with your child, and in addition calms her down for sleep.

Take your child to the library regularly, as a treat. Spend a rainy Saturday afternoon there. Take home different kinds of books—picture books, chapter books, nonfiction books, and poetry. Help your child find books on topics he likes—bugs, trains, puppies, dinosaurs, or monsters. Ask the librarian to suggest books that children your child's age enjoy. Dip into classic children's fiction like *Heidi, Hans Brinker and the Silver Skates*, or *The Wizard of Oz*. Find and share books you enjoyed as a child. Read *Curious George, Madeline*, and *Babar*. And take advantage of the growing number of excellent storytelling, holiday celebration, summer reading clubs, and other programs at libraries, all of which encourage reading by making it a social activity.

When you read to your child, here's how to promote his literacy skills:

- After you read a page, talk about the picture: "Have you ever seen a real rabbit knitting?" "What do you see coming out of the chimney?" "How many hats do you think George will put on his head?" "Oh, doesn't that gingerbread look delicious?"
- Read the name of the author and illustrator of the book. Look for a picture of the author and read the dedication. This way your young child will understand that people create books, and will start to recognize favorite authors.
- Stop in the middle of the story and ask your child to predict what will happen next: "What do you think the Lost Boys will do now?"
- At the end of the story ask questions like "Why did George want to leave home?" "Why did the man always wear a yellow hat?"
- Link the story to your child's own experiences: "Do you think Johnny feels the way you did when Rover disappeared for two days?"
- If a character in the story has the same name as your child (or a brother, friend, or cousin), point to it. "Look, his name is Charlie, just like you, and he writes it just like you write your name."
- As your child begins to show an interest in letters, from time to time point out words that start with the same first letter as his name: "Look, Maggie starts with an *M*, just like the *M* in your name, Mandy." Little by little, point out more letters, or ask your child, "Do you know what letter that is? It's a *D*, the same letter 'Daddy' starts with."

But don't overdo it. Too much "teaching" will interrupt the flow and turn a story into a mindless phonics lesson. If your child is really interested, play a game out of "finding all the *B*s" when the story is over. If she gets distracted after the fourth *B*, drop the game and find something else interesting to do.

DON'T FORGET MATH

Knowing how to read and write is the basis for most academic learning, and many schools rightly stress the goal of every child reading by age nine. That doesn't mean, however, that math learning isn't important.

You can boost your child's math competency by involving her in everyday activities that demand mathematical reasoning. Keep in mind that math is more than addition and subtraction. It also involves recognizing shapes, sorting, measuring, and estimating, as well as comparing, inferring, and predicting. When you draw your child into everyday activities that involve that kind of reasoning, explicitly connect them to math. This will let him know he's building his competency in that subject. "We're doing math," you can say while sorting and pairing a box of buttons ("Big ones go with big ones, small ones with small ones"), or while figuring out how many potatoes to cook for dinner ("Get one for each person in the family. If you can do that, you know how to count and you haven't even started kindergarten!").

The blocks I recommended in chapter 2 are terrific for helping kids learn math (remember that they are geometrical shapes). When your child is building a structure, ask her, "How did you build that?" or "Guess which block I'm looking at?" and then give hints ("It's on the bottom row, next to a round block"). These questions stimulate her to think and talk about the blocks' size, shape, and spatial relationships, says Susan Ohanian, a math teacher.[4]

Here are some other math activities to try:[5]

- Let your three-year-old cross off calendar days to his birthday or to Thanksgiving to teach him to mark time.

- Record your child's growth with pencil marks on the wall to teach him about measurement and comparison.

- Label the sections of an egg carton with the numbers 1 through 12. Give your child seventy-eight beans and ask him to count them into the sections of the carton, according to the numbers. (One bean in the section marked 1, two beans in the section marked 2, and so on.)[6] If the counting is accurate your child will use exactly seventy-eight beans. Can you explain why?

- Count a handful of beans with your child. Then help arrange them in pairs to find out if the number is odd or even. An odd number will have one bean left over and an even number will come out even, with no beans left over. Keep a record of what happens. Ask, "Do you see a pattern?"

Building Competencies in Your School-Age Child

The first idea that pops into your head when you think about boosting your school-age child's competencies is probably helping her with homework. That can be very helpful, but there are many other ways to promote your child's brainpower. Here are some suggestions:

KEEP THE CONVERSATIONS GOING

Talking with you is as important for building your older child's verbal skills as it is for your little one. Encourage your school-age child to tell you about events, experiences, and feelings. If you don't understand what he said, ask him to elaborate. That way he'll learn to give listeners all the information they need to understand. So turn the television off during dinner and use the quiet time together for conversation. Make good use too of the time spent in line at the post office or in the dentist's waiting room.

KEEP READING

Reading at home boosts competencies for kids of all ages. If your children have outgrown your bedtime stories, they can read to themselves, like my friend Nora's son Preston. His daily schedule on the refrigerator has the 8–8:30 P.M. slot before bedtime marked "quiet reading." Or start a "new" reading habit, making reading for pleasure a family affair. Older kids can read to you, or to a little brother or sister.

Many kids need a routine involving at least one adult to spark their interest in reading. I loved reading chapter books like the *Wizard of Oz*, the *Secrets of the NIMH*, and *Tom Sawyer* to my kids when they were nine or ten. Or you can read together. Meredith and I now read our own books every night, side by side, occasionally sharing with the other what we're learning or finding humorous.

- Communicate your expectations primarily by sharing your own enthusiasm. It's not reading for pleasure if you "make" your kids read.
- You might do as literacy learning specialist Lucy Calkins did when her son outgrew his naptime: she allowed him to choose whether to sleep or read during his afternoon rest period. During summer vacation she reads in bed early in the morning and invites her children to join in. "Don't you just love to read first thing?" she asks.[7]
- Make sure your home has lots of different reading materials— newspapers, books, and magazines.

Don't worry if your child seems interested in books that are not classics. As long as they are not morally offensive and don't cause nightmares, it is better for children to read "junk," even comic books, than not to read at all. Suggest, buy, or bring home from the library some better reading material, just in case he runs out of the other stuff. But if your subtle attempts to improve your child's taste fail, don't worry. He's still made a *habit* of reading, and that's what counts.

Most important, show your child that you enjoy reading. Remember that kids "do as you do, not as you say." Studies have shown that the more reading materials in the home, and the more parents read themselves, the better are children's reading skills.[8]

And don't forget that literacy also involves writing. Help your child set up e-mail communication with friends and family, or even revive the ancient practice of writing letters. If you go on vacation, encourage your child to pick out and send postcards to friends. Buy attractive journals, and fancy papers for special letters. Help him find a pen pal—a cousin in another town or an age-mate in another country.

KEEP UP MATH GAMES

Here are some games to play that will teach your school-age child valuable math concepts:

- At the supermarket, encourage your child to estimate—not just guess wildly—the cost of a cart of groceries.
- Talk with your child about some of the numbers she sees in the newspaper or hears on a TV news or science program. "What's the difference between a million and a billion?"
- Ask your nine-year-old sports nut what a .289 batting average means. Challenge her to figure out how many at-bats each player has in a typical game.
- Ask your fifth-grader to calculate whether it's more economical to buy a big container of juice or a six-pack of cans.
- Teach your child how to use a spreadsheet to keep track of how he spends his allowance.
- Browse together through the *Guinness Book of World Records*, which includes many numerical comparisons.

When you play number games, math teachers recommend paying as much attention to your child's thinking as you do to her answer. Once she's old enough for an allowance, you can ask, "If you had pennies,

Drawing a child out in this way is especially valuable when she's given an incorrect answer. Rethinking her steps may lead her toward the correct one, while simultaneously stretching her mathematical thinking abilities. It can be helpful to share your own reasoning skills with your child. Say, "Here's how I figured this out." But don't insist your child do a problem one particular way.

nickels, dimes, and quarters, how many different ways could you pay for a twenty-five-cent brownie?" Then follow up with "How did you come up with that answer?" "What were you thinking about?" "Are there any other possible answers to the question?"

Create a Supportive Environment for Learning

You can indirectly support your child's developing competencies by making sure she has quiet time to study. Most children don't need absolute silence, but television, conversation, or other background noise can be distracting. It isn't easy to keep a small house with other children calm, but try to hold noise and interruptions to a minimum.

Teach Your Child Study Skills

Another way to help your child develop his academic competencies is to teach him how to study. For example, you can

- Encourage him to read instructions carefully and check that he has followed them after he finishes his work. For example, if a science question asked for an answer to the hundredth decimal, teach him to make sure that he has followed the directions precisely.

- Go through a social studies chapter and ask questions to show your child how to check her own understanding as she reads. Point out that she can get clues about the kinds of questions to ask herself from those her teacher asks in class and on tests.
- Teach your child how to organize and learn material by outlining it, and how to make flash cards for memorizing facts.
- Show him how to use a monthly planner in which he lists tests and work due dates, and how to organize his assignments and notes in a notebook so he can find them easily.

When Competence Is Still a Problem

But what if your child is having difficulty with schoolwork despite your efforts to support her intellectual development? Perhaps she is in a highly demanding school, or perhaps it takes her a little longer to catch on than most other kids.

The first step is to discuss your observations with the teacher and ask for advice. Some teachers are grateful to parents who are willing to help a child who has fallen behind. Children occasionally get lost temporarily, and just need a little boost to catch up. A child who is lagging in math, for example, may not have memorized his addition and subtraction facts or the times tables, and simply needs extra practice. Other times the skill deficits are more serious, and a child needs a lot of help.

Don't jump to the conclusion that your child needs a tutor. Sometimes tutoring is the most efficient solution. But for most children, there are less expensive alternatives. For example, some teachers are willing to give a little extra help at lunchtime or after school, or to suggest ways that you, an older child, or a classmate can help. In some classrooms there is an aide or a volunteer who can work with individual or small groups of children. Sometimes teachers can adjust the work to make sure that it is at the right level for your child.

So talk to your child's teacher if he is struggling, and work out a plan. Make sure your child understands that you are trying to support, not punish him. Talk to him about the plan, ask for his suggestions, and see what he's willing to do. That way he will feel some ownership of the plan and some responsibility for it.

Gaining the competencies needed to succeed in school is crucial for becoming a self-motivated learner. But *being* competent is not the only ingredient. To be eager learners, kids also have to *know* they're competent and *believe* they will become competent when they try something new. That's because, where motivation is concerned, beliefs are just as important as reality. In the next chapter I'll show you how to foster your child's confidence in his own competence.

4

Feeling Competent:
As Important as Competence Itself

Hannah scores well on standardized math tests, and in class discussions she seems to understand the math. But when her fifth-grade teacher invites her to join an advanced math group, Hannah refuses. "The work will be too hard," she explains. The teacher is not entirely surprised, because Hannah shows other signs of lacking self-confidence. Sometimes when the class is learning a new concept, Hannah is easily discouraged. And occasionally she turns in homework with the harder problems left blank.

Hannah is competent, but she *feels* incompetent. She doesn't really think she can do difficult work.

If feelings of competency are a powerful engine driving a child's desire to try, feelings of *in*competence are like sand in the motivational gas tank. After all, if a student believes she is incompetent, as Hannah does, it doesn't make sense to persist when she runs into difficulty.

Research has shown that children's *beliefs* about their academic competence and whether they expect their efforts to lead to success are at least as important as their actual competence. Whether people *think* they can succeed influences their effort more than whether they actually *can*. As Stanford University psychologist Albert Bandura says, "The stronger [people's] belief in their capabilities, the stronger and more persistent are their efforts."[1] It makes sense: if you know you won't succeed, why try?

Making sure that your child has the skills to succeed in school is, therefore, only half the battle. You also need to make sure your child believes that he can increase his competence to meet new challenges. This chapter is about how to maximize your child's *belief* that she is competent and can become even more so. It's a vital component of self-motivation to learn.

All Children Are Vulnerable

As you would expect, children who have done poorly in school for a long time often expect to fail, sometimes on work they could do well if they tried. But the "I can't do it" feeling can haunt *any* student, even a highly skilled one.

Surprisingly, research has shown that gifted children, especially bright girls, are especially vulnerable to underestimating their abilities. Psychologist Deborah Phillips found in a study of high-achieving ninth-graders that 20 percent grossly underestimated their competencies. The effects were serious: not only did these students expect less from themselves than did the other high achievers, they also tended to shy away from difficult work. And they felt more anxious about tests and grades, and were more likely to believe that parents and teachers considered them "not very bright." Like the other ninth-graders in the study, they were in the top 25 percent of their class. Who knows what they might have accomplished without these rocks of self-doubt weighing them down?[2]

Phillips also made a startling discovery: girls composed 66 percent of the students studied, but 100 percent of those who underestimated their competency![3] (This finding may surprise some, but not feminists, who have always argued that modern society gives many women the message they are less capable and intelligent than men.)

There are several reasons why bright kids may be underconfident. Kids who excel in one subject sometimes feel incompetent when another subject is comparatively more difficult for them. A gifted writer, for example, may consider herself dumb in math, despite perfectly respectable competence, because math requires more effort from her.

High-achieving students also may feel incompetent because they have unrealistically high standards. They may be praised so frequently for their intellectual prowess that they begin to think adults expect superhuman performance from them, and no matter what they do, they will fall short.

Highly competent kids also often get used to being "at the top" of the class and may lose confidence when they are not. For example, a child who is very successful in a regular class may suffer a crisis in self-confidence when she becomes "average" by moving to a class of gifted children.

Although no child is immune, underconfidence usually doesn't crop up until the upper elementary grades. Some young children are very timid and anxious about trying anything new, but few kids have serious self-confidence problems before the second or third grade.

In fact, my research has found that in the early grades, most children *over*estimate their academic competencies, expecting to succeed even when they lack necessary skills. Indeed, nearly all the kindergarten children in my studies usually claim to be the smartest in their class! By second grade, however, most children begin to pay attention to classroom feedback. They judge their competence by their grades or their reading group assignment, for example, and by sixth grade the self-confidence of many children has dropped dramatically.

Whether your child is high- or low-achieving, successful or failing, average or gifted, he may need help from you in one or more subjects to believe that he will succeed if he tries. It's wise to be on the lookout for signs that your child doesn't appreciate his own competence in some nook or cranny of his academic life (and you should do all you can to prevent his self-doubt). Let's look now at how you can do just that.

Helping Your Child Believe She Can Succeed

Recently I attended a school reunion and made up a trivia quiz, which I read to my old schoolmates sitting at a wooden picnic table in the campground where we had gathered. I enjoyed reading the quiz questions aloud and laughed along with everyone else at the answers. But it wasn't until a friend said to me as we drove away, "Your trivia quiz was wonderful!" that I knew for sure that it had been a hit. I felt a rush of pride and pleasure, along with increased confidence in my ability to entertain. Even adults like me sometimes need feedback from others to appreciate their competencies!

PROVIDE POSITIVE INFORMATIONAL FEEDBACK

You can do for your child what my friend did for me. Praise her for her achievements, so that she feels competent about the skills and knowledge she acquires.

"Why should I have to tell my child she's competent?" you might wonder. "Don't kids already know?"

Not always. When kids are small, they usually don't need adult help to know what they can do, because most of their new skills have built-in feedback. When their shoes stay tied for a few seconds, the tricycle moves as they push the pedals, or the puzzle pieces fit neatly into the frame, young children automatically feel competent.

Competency feedback is sometimes built into older children's activities too. When your daughter's bike doesn't fall over, her computer program works, or she finishes a book harder or longer than the ones she usually reads, she will know she's accomplished something. But the older kids get, the more complex are the tasks they do, and the more they need adult feedback to appreciate their skill development. For example, children may not be able to gauge the progress they've made in grasping scientific principles or improving their writing style. Your son may not realize that his ideas are creative, his essay is touching, his science project is well designed, or his explanations for solving a set of math problems are clear until someone tells him so.

That's where parents (and teachers) come in. Positive informational feedback nourishes your child's feelings of competence. The more specific or informational your feedback, the better. General praise like "Good job!" or "Way to go!" warms kids up with positive feelings. But comments that tell your child exactly what she's accomplished are better, because they identify her competencies.

Since knowledge and skills are often like blocks built on each other, knowing precisely what she *can* do helps your child approach her next academic step. "I now know how to write good sentences; the teacher told me I just need to learn to put them together to make a paragraph," she might think, or "I know how to add; the teacher says multiplying is a faster way to do lots of additions." So to your general praise, "Good work," or "Great job!" add specific comments like

- "I can read every letter in your name!"
- "Your drawing of the human heart is just as good as the one in the textbook."
- "Your story is very vivid! I can see the meadow you're describing."
- "You got all those problems right. You've learned to do long division with remainders and you're only eight years old!"

I realize you don't always have the time or the skills to give your child specific informational feedback. When your five-year-old brings you a scribbled picture and you're busy making dinner, maybe you can only glance at it and comment that it looks just like Daddy. And as kids

My friend Susan brought home to me the importance of positive, informational feedback one day when we were jogging on the beach. "I went to Radcliffe," she said, "but the entire time I was there I wondered whether they'd accepted me because of my father's contribution to the school's endowment." Had someone at the college explained to Susan that she'd been accepted because her high school teachers praised her work or because her interest in Celtic literature was valuable to the Harvard community, she might have felt much more confident.

get older, they start outstripping us. I can't make heads or tails out of some of Meredith's science work now that she's in high school, so I don't say much more than, "I like the colors in your graph." But even when you aren't sure exactly what your child has accomplished, let him know where you see his strengths:

- "You've always been good at word problems."
- "You're really an outstanding writer."
- "Your computer skills are truly amazing."

FOCUS ON YOUR CHILD'S ROLE

Sometimes kids fail to build a sense of competence because they deny their own responsibility for success. For example, they may say that the work was really easy, that they were lucky, or that they succeeded because they had help or worked harder than everyone else.

You can help ward off this self-deprecation by specifically mentioning your child's role when you praise him. Point out the factors within his control—such as his concentration, persistence, or organization—that led to his success. That way you'll build your child's confidence by focusing on strengths that he can draw on in the future. Here are some examples of comments that will help your child take responsibility for her own success, bolstering her belief that she is competent and can become more so:

- "You worked so carefully, and stuck with this even when you were tired of doing it. Your persistence really paid off!"
- "You really worked hard on that story—you should feel proud of yourself."
- "The extra research you did on the Internet really helped you get on top of this pollution topic."
- "Remember how you struggled with that hard chapter in your science book until you finally understood it? If you keep plugging away at your math the same way, I bet you'll figure that out too."

COMMUNICATE *YOUR* CONFIDENCE IN YOUR CHILD

University of Pittsburgh researcher Sharon Nelson–Le Gall remembers the day she came home from second grade in tears. She was assigned to write an entire sentence in cursive script by Monday! Nelson–Le Gall had struggled so hard to learn to connect each letter in script; now she was worried she wouldn't know how to stop connecting letters at the end of each word. When her mother pointed out she already had learned to print words in a sentence, she calmed down. "My mother reminded me I already knew how much space came between printed words," she recalls. "She made it very obvious to me, and I thought, 'Yes, I can do this, too.'"[4]

Sometimes kids simply need us to remind them what they already know to give them the necessary confidence to take the next step. If your child is discouraged, go back to the part of the work he was able to do. If he is struggling to tie his shoe, for example, but missed several holes, you can say, "You got the lace through these three holes, so I know you can get it through the others." Similarly, if he's having trouble finishing a page of math calculations, you might point out to him,

"You've already done almost half! You sure seem to know what you're doing." If your daughter claims the spelling words are too hard, comment, "But you only missed one word on your spelling test last week, and these are very similar."

When your child seems anxious about a major assignment or test, remind her of strategies that worked before:

- "You planned well for your social studies report, and the teacher commented how well organized and thorough it was. I'm sure you can do the same for your science project."
- "Remember last year how you said beginning to study for tests a few days ahead of time worked well for you? Why don't you try that again?"

Sometimes all that's needed are a few words of encouragement, like "I know you can do it," or a challenge: "I bet you can finish that chapter before dinner if you really concentrate."

But express your confidence only when you are sure your child *can* achieve the goal. It's maddening to have someone tell you that you can do something when you're certain you can't.

ACKNOWLEDGE DIFFICULTY

If "But this is so easy!" pops into your head when your child is having difficulty with her schoolwork, don't say it. Saying a task is easy won't make it so. Think how you would feel if your neighbor walked in to find you baffled by a tax form, and said, "Oh, that's so easy!" Far from giving you confidence, such a remark would probably make you want to throw the form in her face.

Similarly, telling a struggling child that his schoolwork is easy won't reassure him, despite your good intentions. More likely, you'll increase his discouragement and anxiety, because difficulty with "easy" work makes people feel much more incompetent than does difficulty with hard work. Rather than discouraging him, agreeing that the work is hard will validate his feelings.

Of course, simply agreeing that work is hard won't raise your child's confidence all by itself. Follow your validating comments with encouragement, or even better, constructive suggestions. Think how you'd feel if your neighbor instead said, "I had a hard time with that one too, but I figured it out eventually. Here, let me show you some tricks." Wouldn't you sigh with relief, and feel immediately confident that you will mail your taxes before midnight after all? Even "I agree, this is a hard one. But it's a lot like the form you filled out last quarter, so I'm sure you'll figure it out," would be encouraging.

POINT OUT SUCCESSFUL MODELS

Sometimes you can give your child courage by pointing out kids the same age who have done what she needs to try. When I taught swimming as a college student I occasionally pointed out one child's accomplishment to another. "Sarah swam the width of the pool and she's smaller than you. I bet you can too," I might say. At the very least, this gave the child who was hesitating to jump in confidence that nothing terrible would happen when she ventured away from the side of the pool.

Use this strategy carefully, however. Pointing out another child's success can also set up a competition that your child will expect to lose. Then he'll be even less willing to try. There's no simple rule for predicting when it will help to point out peers' accomplishments. You just have to know your child well and observe her reactions sensitively.

You can use yourself as a model too, but be credible. My father used to tell us frequently how many miles he walked through the snow to get to school (uphill both ways, we always added). His claims didn't make walking to school in Tacoma's daily drizzle any easier for me. So try to limit yourself to believable stories. "We did a little algebra in elementary school too. At first it seemed hard, but eventually it started to make sense, and I remember really liking it."

Don't unwittingly use yourself as a negative model. Stay away from comments like

- "I never could do math either," or
- "I've always had a problem with writer's block."

Rather than encouraging your child to try, such statements provide a great excuse to give up. It's all right to share difficulties you had as a student, but make sure that the moral of the story is that you stuck with it and persistence paid off.

BREAK TASKS INTO DOABLE PIECES

Mrs. Schmidt found Jeremy, her sixth-grader, asleep on his bedroom floor when she came home from work. Strewn around him were all kinds of materials—maps, a textbook, a binder, instruction sheets, colored pencils, and more. The cause of his sudden fatigue, it turns out, was the assignment of a social studies report on ancient Egypt. The report had to include maps, pictures, news clippings, and information on several topics outlined by the teacher. Jeremy didn't know where to start. Just looking at the instructions made him sleepy. "I'll never be able to get this done, Mom," he moaned at dinner. "Mr. Davis must think we're in high school to give us something like this," he wailed. "I'm only twelve!"

Stanford psychologist Albert Bandura and his colleague Dale Schunk thought overwhelmed students like Jeremy might feel better if they could break their work into small chunks. To test their theory, they gave three groups of elementary school children seven sets of subtraction problems to do over seven sessions. They told the first group to work on one set each session, and the second group to finish all the work by the end of the final sessions. The last group was given no goal, but simply told to work on the problems.

The result? The first group of kids estimated they would do more problems correctly than the other two groups, and they did just that. Even something as straightforward as a set of subtraction problems seemed more manageable to children when the task was broken down into smaller units.[5]

Adults sometimes use this technique to motivate themselves to finish what seems like a monstrous job. "Okay, I'll read one chapter of this student's doctoral thesis every day, and then I'll be finished by Wednesday," I tell myself. Or "If I get through my business bills before dinner, I'll only have the house bills to do afterwards."

You can use this "break it into chunks" method to help your child if she feels overwhelmed and paralyzed by a complicated assignment. Breaking the task into small steps will help her overcome her fear of not knowing where to start, and distract her attention from the intimidating size and complexity of the work. And achieving each of the multiple milestones will give her continual feelings of accomplishment and competence. For example,

- If your daughter is put off by word problems at the end of her math homework, suggest she forget about them and do the computation problems first, and then take a break. After the break, point out that the word problems ask her to do essentially the same kind of calculations she has been doing.
- When a long book dismays your third-grader, help him set daily chapter goals that will seem less daunting. Contribute to his sense of competence by acknowledging him for meeting each day's goal.

And let's not forget poor Jeremy, last seen panicking about his Egypt report. What could his mother do? First, she could help him list sections of the report and develop a plan for completing each section. (It's a good idea to build extra time into a schedule, in case a section takes longer than expected or other homework is unexpectedly heavy.) She should also encourage Jeremy to forget about the end product and concentrate on one section at a time. Thus, in any one day he might read two chapters and take notes, or draw a map, or search for pictures on the Internet. Each of these bits will seem more manageable to him than a ten-page, multidimensional report.

In addition to increasing short-term motivation, helping your child break a big assignment into manageable pieces will arm him with strategies for the future. In the spring when he has to do a science report, Jeremy will be able to structure the new assignment himself, relying on what he learned when his mom helped him plan his Egypt report in the fall.

Criticism and Sympathy: Their Counterintuitive Effects

My kids often brought me their essays and term papers to read. I'm pretty obsessive-compulsive, and used to circle every mistake I saw in red, writing questions and comments in the margin. I didn't want to discourage my children, so I always tried to give them positive feedback too, suppressing my tendency to hold unrealistically high standards for anyone remotely related to me, including our three cats. But perhaps because my kids' early schooling took place during the heyday of the self-esteem movement, I sometimes worried that my criticism would turn them off to writing.

Quite the opposite occurred. Far from throwing cold water on my kids' desire to write, my criticism appears to have nourished it. Jeff wrote a popular column in his high school newspaper, and Zach wrote for his college paper. Meredith likes to spend free time writing fantasy tales *à la* Tolkien.

CRITICISM CAN BUILD CONFIDENCE

My experience with my own children illustrates the counterintuitive research findings that criticism can make people feel competent. In one study of twenty fifth- to ninth-grade classrooms, for example, researchers found that students whose teachers criticized the quality of their work (but not the questions they asked) felt more competent and confident in math than students in classrooms where criticism was rare.[6] (The teachers' criticism was of course constructive, not mean or destructive.)

UCLA psychologists George Barker and Sandra Graham showed that by about age ten or eleven children understand the implications of critical feedback. Kids in their study watched a videotape of two students doing work equally well. The teacher was critical of one child ("Come on now, what are you doing? The correct answer is nine") and gave neutral information ("No, that is not the correct answer") to the other. The kids watching the videotape concluded that the child criticized by the teacher was more intelligent than the child the teacher didn't criticize.[7]

How could criticism make children feel more rather than less confident? The answer is that when we criticize people, the underlying message is that we think they *can* do better, that they have control over their achievement. When we don't think people can do any better, we don't get angry or want to criticize. For example, we don't get mad and honk at a disabled person still crossing the street after the light turns green, but we might get angry and even yell out the window at an apparently able-bodied person holding up traffic while he ambles slowly across the road. When teachers and parents give critical feedback, they send the message that they believe the child can improve. A teacher won't "waste" criticism on a student she doesn't believe capable of using it. This is probably why I am encouraged when the teacher corrects me in the dance class I take at the YMCA. In addition to giving me useful feedback, it tells me she believes I can improve. When she ignores me, I feel like she's given up hope!

I'm not suggesting you start pouring criticism on your kid like syrup on pancakes. But constructive criticism, balanced with positive feedback, can boost your child's feelings of competence. When, in a calm and friendly tone, you give specific criticism aimed at helping your

Try mixing praise and criticism ("commendations and recommendations"):

- "Your points are very clear, but it's not clear how they're connected to each other. It would help to add transitions between your paragraphs."
- "You use the correct tense, but your verbs don't always agree with the subjects."
- "You've got the first set of problems right, but not the second set. You need to check it over more carefully, because I think most of your mistakes are just careless errors."

child correct and improve his work, you convey that you are confident your child can correct and improve. Lack of success, you imply, will come from not trying hard enough, or from an ineffective strategy.

SYMPATHY CAN UNDERMINE CONFIDENCE

Sympathy presents another apparent paradox. Wouldn't you think it would make your child feel better if she was having difficulty? But research shows that people feel sympathy when they think a problem or failure is beyond a person's control. That's why you're likely to feel more sympathetic than angry toward the handicapped person holding up traffic at a crosswalk. Similarly, we feel sympathy for a colleague who gets behind at work because she is sick, but not for one who is lazy.

So if your child did poorly on a spelling test and you say, "Don't feel bad, that's okay," you risk sending her the message that you don't think she had any control over her performance, and that she couldn't have done better.

Rather than sympathizing with your child if she does poorly, empathize:

- "That grade must be disappointing."
- "I can understand why you feel badly about doing poorly on your science test."

But after that, turn her attention immediately to analyzing the cause and finding a remedy:

- "Any thoughts about why you got a D?"
- "Do you have any idea about what to do next time, to make sure you do better?"
- "Did you make a lot of silly mistakes, or are you having trouble understanding?"
- "Do you think it would help to talk to the teacher about the problems you're having? Maybe he'll have some tips for studying next time?"
- "Would it help if I read over your book report before you turn it in next time?"

Make sure your underlying message is that you believe your child can do better: all she needs is more effort, a different strategy, or perhaps a little help.

Nurturing Confidence When the Work *Is* Too Hard

My friend Barbara's daughter was assigned to write a research report and make a visual presentation on Harriet Tubman. Leah was supposed to cover Tubman's early life (birth, family life, incidents that had an impact on her adult work), her contribution to history, and the lessons her life teaches. She was also told to compare and contrast Tubman with another famous person, and compose a journal entry Tubman might have written about an incident. The visual presentation was to include a diorama depicting a significant event in Tubman's life, a collage, and a timeline. What an interesting assignment! Unfortunately, Leah was then in the second grade.

Barbara's experience was by no means unique. My sister-in-law, Susie, showed me the complicated diorama about the Chumash Indians her son Andy was assigned to make in the fourth grade. (Susie ended up doing most of it.) I've heard similar stories from countless parents. These days many schools involve parents in their children's education by assigning projects that are so difficult children could never do them alone. Science fair projects have become a bugbear of many families; I have a friend who actually canceled a vacation so her husband would be home to help their son with his project.

The practice of assigning homework that children cannot possibly do on their own is indefensible, except in rare cases when the goal is to promote some meaningful interaction between children and parents. Most parents have already graduated from elementary school and have little to gain from doing their children's homework. And children learn nothing when their parents do their work.

CHANGE THE TASK

If an assignment seems way over your child's head, encourage her to clarify what the teacher expects. Sometimes children misunderstand what the teacher is requiring. If you still think the work is too difficult for your child, share your opinion with the teacher, especially if this is not the first time. (Make sure your child agrees that the work is beyond him; sometimes parents underestimate what children can do.)

Also make sure *you're* not giving your child work that's too hard. Sometimes parents overestimate their children's competence and give them tasks that engender feelings of incompetence and frustration. Whether teaching your child to recognize letters, play the violin, or identify star constellations, you'll need to notice the cues she gives you. It's fine to set high standards and have high expectations, but that doesn't mean asking children to do things they can't do. In our eagerness to help our children face today's competitive world, we sometimes push them too fast and become frustrated when they are unwilling partners in our ambitious plans. A reluctant child may not be lazy or defiant; she may simply lack the necessary skills or maturity.

If your child seems stumped by a puzzle, a science experiment, a building project, or a book you suggested, suggest a change in the activity. This needn't be humiliating. Simply say something like "Let's try one of these other puzzles first, and work up to that one." Or "Now that I think about it, I was several years older than you when I read that book. No wonder it seems hard to you."

Clubs and organizations also sometimes give children inappropriately difficult tasks, especially when the group has a broad age range. If activities are consistently over your child's head, it might be necessary to change scout troops, move her to a different computer class, or postpone the religious instruction class for a year.

Above all, make sure your child feels comfortable telling you he's having difficulty. Listen first. Don't dismiss his concerns or launch into a burst of encouragement before you have heard him out. Sometimes our own desires are so obvious that our kids are afraid to disappoint us. They hide their frustration and anxieties, as well as their feelings of incompetence. If your child isn't eager to continue a computer class or piano lessons, you may need to ask some questions the next time you're relaxed together to find out what the problem is.

CHANGE THE DEFINITION OF SUCCESS:
SET REALISTIC GOALS

Caroline studied diligently, as she always does, for a difficult science test. However, she didn't have time to ask her teacher about a few concepts that still confused her. When the test came back, Caroline was relieved to find B+ at the top. That evening she happily showed it to her dad.

"A B+?" he said sympathetically. "What went wrong, honey?" Like a popped balloon, Caroline's pride suddenly deflated into humiliation.

Caroline's dad had, in effect, defined success for her as an A. Anything short of that grade represented failure. Such high expectations are a heavy burden, even for a good student. You have a strong influence on your child's standards, so use it to help him define success as meeting the "just-right challenge" I described in previous chapters—work that is demanding but doable. When her performance dips occasionally, cut her a little slack.

Imagine, for example, that your daughter has been getting right only eight or nine out of twenty weekly spelling words. You can encourage her to try to get twelve correct on the next test. If she meets that target, celebrate it as though she's won the World Cup. Even though twelve out of twenty may be a failing grade, it's a major accomplishment for her. When she meets this goal, encourage her to raise the bar, perhaps to fourteen or fifteen. Remember that learning is like Aesop's turtle and hare race: what matters is not how fast you go, but whether you advance steadily until you finish.

Similarly, if your son is getting Ds and an occasional F, you might propose he try for "no grade lower than a C." If your daughter wants to attend college but got two Cs on her report card, encourage her to aim for all As and Bs.

Los Angeles psychologist Wendy Mogel describes a family that had to change its definition of success for the sake of their daughter's mental health. The young girl was only an average student in a high-achieving family, so her parents took her to tutoring five days a week. "She was a perfectly normal girl of average intelligence with lots of skills, but in a school that was far too academically rigorous for her," recalls Mogel. The daughter "was wondering if she was brain damaged, or retarded." Mogel convinced the girl's parents to change schools and stop the tutoring, and soon the girl was thriving.[8]

Both short-term and long-term goals are useful, but consider your child's age. For young children a semester grade is too far off to think about; it may be more productive to focus their attention on the next test, report, essay, or homework assignment. The younger the child, the closer should be the goal.

If your child tells you about his overly unrealistic ambitions, you needn't automatically gush wholehearted enthusiasm. Don't say, "That would be great if you win the science fair." Instead, suggest something more realistic, like "That would be nice, but I'll be delighted if you get to the finals." Or, even better: "It would be wonderful to win a ribbon, but what impresses me is that you worked hard, and that *you* know that you did a good job on your science project."

"But I thought we were supposed to have high expectations for our kids!" you may object. "Why should we lower our standards? Won't they achieve more if we expect more? Don't high expectations demonstrate our strong faith in their ability?"

Yes, the sky is still the limit. But setting and reaching intermediate goals will give your child a sense of accomplishment and competence, which in turn will nourish her motivation. Defining success that's realistically achievable fuels her desire to keep studying and learning. As

---

When kids play, they often adjust their goals naturally to ensure success. For example, if toddlers find that the puzzle pieces aren't fitting into the form, they may simply switch to piling the pieces into a tower or lining them up like a train. Older children occasionally change the rules of a game to improve their chance of success. "Let's move the line up so we can stand closer," an eight-year-old might suggest when only a few rubber darts have found the target, let alone the bull's eye. It's not easy to change schoolwork goals so rapidly, but you should strive for similar flexibility.

your child gains confidence in her academic abilities, you can help her raise the bar.

BEWARE OF THE CURSE OF THE PERFECT SIBLING

Sometimes siblings are the source of unrealistically high standards for children. Teachers often contribute to the problem. "Oh, I had your sister Margaret in my class," a child hears over and over from teachers. "How is she doing? She was such an outstanding student." Or, more explicitly, "I'm expecting great things from the sister of Margaret Brown!"

Don't compare your child to a brother or sister or cousin who had a 4.0 GPA, won a basketball scholarship to UCLA, or founded a world-wide children's crusade to bring peace to the Balkans while still in middle school. Frequent mention of their siblings' accomplishments can haunt children with a feeling of inadequacy, no matter how well they do.

To avoid the sibling effect, tailor your expectations to fit each child individually. Praise your son for improving his algebra grade from a C− to a B as much as you praise your daughter for making the honor roll. In addition, give your children many opportunities to develop their skills and talents, so that every child has a chance to feel very competent in something.

Encourage Your Daughter in Math and Science

- "I was never as good at math as my brother."
- "Every time your mother tries to balance the checkbook, she messes it up."
- "Don't feel badly if it's hard for you. Girls aren't usually very good at math."

Comments like these are among the social messages that explain why girls, on average, see themselves as less competent than boys in math and science, even though they perform just as well. Make sure you don't unwittingly reinforce the cultural stereotype of boys as math whizzes and science nerds, and girls as giggly and helpless when it comes to algebra and frog dissection.

Studies have shown that parents play an important role in girls' relatively low opinions of their math and science competencies. Research has found, for example, that parents tend to judge their daughters' math ability lower than their sons', expect them to be less successful in math, and are less likely to envision them in a math career. University of Michigan psychologist Jacque Eccles (née Parsons) and her colleagues also report that parents spend more time working or playing at the computer with boys than with girls, and they encourage boys more often to take up math or science activities.[9]

Girls get the message: Eccles found that girls' judgments of their own math competence were influenced more by their parents' opinions than by their own grades or test scores in math. My doctoral student at UCLA, Patricia Byler, recently found also that parents who themselves enjoyed and felt confident at math believed their girls were competent and liked math. And guess what? They were right. As in Eccles's studies, parents' perceptions of their girls' feelings about math predicted girls' own feelings, more than did girls' actual performance in math.[10]

You don't have to pretend to love math and science. But don't broadcast negative feelings either. Beware also of sending more subtle messages. My friend Nancy once told me her husband helped their children with math homework and she helped them with reading and writing. In and of itself such a division of labor is harmless. But her husband also took charge of the family budget, bills, banking, and financial planning, while Nancy shopped, cooked, cleaned, and tended to everyone's emotional life. Just about everything that went on in this household reinforced the view that men are good at "hard" subjects and women at "softer" ones.

If this is the pattern in your family, make sure to balance it with positive messages to your children about girls' ability to succeed in math and science. Your sons and daughters deserve the same high expectations; help them both to develop plenty of competence and confidence.

Now that you've seen how to boost your child's competence and his *belief* in his competence, let's look at the second crucial component of loving learning: a sense of autonomy. In the next chapter you'll learn how and when to give your child both choice and responsibility.

5

Autonomy: Giving Your Child Choice and Responsibility

Nagging and yelling rang out constantly at the Millers' house. "I'm sick and tired of trying to get you to do your homework," Natasha Miller would blurt out impatiently to nine-year-old Vanessa. "You're just lazy and don't want to work."

Vanessa had failed two subjects on her last report card, but Natasha and her husband, Rick, could see that their negative comments and nagging were only making matters worse. So in the beginning of Vanessa's fourth-grade year, they decided to attend a parenting class. There they learned that their constant reminders were a way of taking over responsibility for their daughter's homework. They were making Vanessa feel that any studying she did was for her parents' sake.

The Millers decided to stop nagging and to give Vanessa responsibility for her own work. The following Saturday morning at breakfast Natasha and Rick made their daughter a proposal: they would agree to stop nagging her. In exchange, Vanessa would start her homework every night by 7:00 P.M., show Natasha or Rick her completed homework, and earn a C or better for every subject on her report card. She also agreed to ask her parents for help with homework whenever she needed it. "Your schoolwork is for your benefit," Rick said, "and doing it is up to you."

After some discussion, Vanessa also agreed that if any night she didn't complete her homework, she would start it the next day as soon as she got home, skipping the TV show she usually watched before dinner.

The first night of the new plan Vanessa started working halfheartedly on her homework just before bedtime. Her parents said nothing, even though Natasha could barely hold herself back and told Rick she had misgivings about the new plan. At 8:20 P.M. Vanessa quit halfway through her math and started playing with the dog. Her parents said nothing. Natasha fell asleep repeating the mantra, "I'm not going to nag, I'm not going to nag."

The next day, when Vanessa sat down in front of the TV, Natasha merely pointed to the refrigerator where they had posted their agreement. Vanessa grumbled and went to her room.

But slowly during that fourth-grade year, Vanessa started changing. Some nights she did all of her homework; other nights her parents had to remind her to turn off the TV. A few times she asked for help with her math. For their part, Natasha and Rick looked for chances to be positive: they praised Vanessa's excellent drawing and her work on a social studies project, and congratulated her whenever she got at least a C grade. At their teacher-parent conference in January, Vanessa's teacher said she was completing her assignments more often. By spring, Vanessa was doing her homework on her own, and her grades had started to improve. She was even helping her younger brother learn to read.

"I felt relieved," remembers Natasha. "I had put too much energy into trying to control her. Now she was in charge. I felt good about that, and I could tell she felt good too."[1]

The Millers praised Vanessa's efforts, but they didn't use bribes or rewards to manipulate her motivation (although losing the TV show was like a punishment). They had realized that trying to control children makes them fight back, and that making them responsible for their own learning promotes their internal motivation.

That's because autonomy—the feeling that you're acting of your own accord—is another necessary ingredient of loving learning. It's probably no surprise to you that people like having control over their own lives. Perhaps that's why the cry in that Anacin commercial of the 1960s—"Mother, please, I'd rather do it myself!"—became such a popular punch line: it underscored the universality of the human drive for self-determination. What you may not know, however, is that research has also shown decisively that people enjoy learning more when they feel they're studying of their own volition rather than because they're pressured to do so.

You've probably seen this drive for autonomy in iron-willed kids who have just acquired a new skill. Try, for example, to feed a baby who's just learned to use a spoon. "No, mine!" she wails, pushing your hand away. Or try to tie the shoes of a five-year-old who's just learned to tie them herself. "I want to do it!" she cries. "Let me!" Psychologist John Watson found that even eight-week-old infants smiled and cooed vigorously when they caused mobiles to move or make noise.[2]

Autonomy is also important because it enables kids to feel pride in their own achievement. If you control or even help your child too much, she may feel grateful, or relieved not to have failed, but she can't claim success as her own.

Adults are the same; we too want to be in charge of our own work. Have you ever noticed how the same activity is more fun when you freely choose it than when it is mandatory? Take the phrase "reading for pleasure," which implies that reading is enjoyable when we choose to do it, while required course reading isn't. That's why my friend Carole, who's in her forties, is rereading classics like *The Scarlet Letter* and *Jane Eyre*. It's not that she wants to recapture her youthful enjoyment, since she found these books oppressive when she had to read them in high school. But now, because she's reading them of her own volition, she enjoys them tremendously.

Indeed, adults (and kids) often resent people who try to control them more than they believe necessary. That's why you may, for example, resent an overbearing boss and goof off when she's not around (as kids do when a controlling teacher leaves the classroom).

Of course, loosening the reins on your child is easier said than done. If he's not trying in school, the natural response is to give him less autonomy, not more. Even when your child *is* trying, giving up control can be hard, perhaps because you feel a child's education is too important to take such a risk. Or maybe your parents brought you up with strict controls, which feel right to you.

But cracking down on our children squelches their feelings of self-determination and in the long run does more harm than good.

"In a lot of families there's a self-fulfilling prophecy," says psychologist Richard Ryan. "Parents say, 'He only works when I yell at him to do it,' and I think, 'Well, yeah, I'm not surprised, because all that yelling has killed any sense the work is theirs to do.'"[3]

Giving Your Child Control Fosters Self-Motivation to Learn

Wendy Grolnick discovered the value of giving children control when she studied a group of mothers demonstrating toys to their one-year-olds. Grolnick noticed that some of the moms, whom she called "supportive," helped their children occasionally—for example, by holding a toy still so their babies could play with it. Most of the time, however, these mothers simply let their children play the way they wanted. In contrast, the other mothers were more controlling. "No, play with it this way," they'd say, moving their child's hand to a part of a toy, or "Do it like this."

Next Grolnick gave all the children a new set of interesting toys (such as cobbler's benches) to play with alone, telling them to "make it work." The babies whose mothers had simply helped them persisted in trying to make the new toys work. But the babies whose mothers had been more controlling tried for a while, then gave up. In other words, the kids who were allowed some autonomy had developed stronger self-motivation to master the task.[4]

Autonomy fosters self-motivation in school-age kids too. Study after study shows that students whose teachers give them some choice and control over their learning become more self-motivated than kids whose teachers direct their every move.[5]

One study of inner-city students showed how test scores can rise when teachers promote autonomy. Psychologist Richard DeCharms gave 1,200 fifth-graders the Iowa Test of Basic Skills in the spring. The following summer, he trained sixteen sixth-grade teachers at a week-long retreat to give their students more control over their learning by helping them to set personal goals, keep track of what they learned, and evaluate their own progress. Students in the classes of sixteen other sixth-grade teachers who were not trained served as the control group. At the end of their sixth-grade year, DeCharms retested the 1,200 children. The kids whose teachers had received the autonomy training gained almost half a year grade equivalent more than the students in the control group. Even more striking is the finding that the high school graduation rate was higher among the six hundred "self-determining" students![6]

Another study showed how even seemingly trivial amounts of choice can warm up children's enthusiasm. Students were allowed to choose which three of six puzzles to work on. This modest choice proved significant: these students persisted longer and expressed more interest in the puzzles than another group of students, for whom the experimenters had chosen which three puzzles they worked on.[7]

Other studies have shown that kids' feelings of autonomy within the family affect both their motivation and their achievement. Grolnick and Ryan interviewed 114 parents of elementary school students. The psychologists found that some parents had a "democratic" style, allowing their kids to choose when and how to do their homework, for

A fourth-grade teacher once complained to me that her students rarely finished their writing assignments. I wasn't surprised, because the teacher determined everything they did: every day the students read a story in their reading book and answered five end-of-the-chapter questions. I suggested the teacher instead let her students choose from three writing assignments (all of which would teach them the same skills). So she told them they could (1) write a new ending to the story, (2) make up their own questions and exchange them with a classmate, or (3) answer the five questions at the end of the chapter. The effect was immediate and dramatic: I watched a previously lethargic class race through the story so they could choose and complete their writing assignments.

example, or to decide which family chores they would do. Other parents in the study tended to control their kids' behavior through bribes and rewards. (One mother, for instance, offered her son sports equipment if he earned As in school, and a father made his child stay inside after school if he earned any grades below C on his report card.)

Next the researchers asked the children's teachers to rate their students' self-motivation. According to their teachers, the kids whose parents had a more democratic style at home were more interested in their schoolwork. They also earned better grades and scored higher on achievement tests. "The more kids feel controlled," explains Ryan, "the less motivated they are."[8]

Promoting Your Child's Autonomy

Once I saw a teacher extinguish a five-year-old's enthusiasm for coloring by pointing out that he hadn't followed the directions at the bottom of the page to "color the bear brown." The little boy had done that, but he'd committed the serious offense of coloring the bear's tongue red!

While this example is extreme, it's not a far cry from the traditional American classroom, where kids are usually told what to do, and when and how to do it. Teachers often spend an inordinate amount of time dictating details, like where to put your name, what color pen to use, and how many pages to write.

While you probably can't change the way your child's teacher teaches, you can have a great impact on your child's self-motivation by allowing a measure of autonomy—some choice and control—at home.

You can often, for example, make choices explicit. When you are playing with your toddler, ask,

- "Which of these puzzles would you like to try?"
- "Why don't you choose the book I read you tonight?"
- "Do you want to play the memory game or the counting game?"

When your child is in preschool or early elementary school, let her decide what she takes for lunch (or let her choose among several healthy options). If there's a choice within your price range, let her pick out her own Halloween costume, lunch box, and umbrella. Make suggestions when you go to the library or bookstore, and help your child find books that interest him. But let him choose which books he takes home.

PROVIDING CHOICE WITHIN A FRAMEWORK

Keep in mind that autonomy doesn't mean permissiveness. Studies show that children need a clear, well-defined structure of rules and consequences. It's within that framework that you want to give your child age-appropriate choices.

The pitfalls of extreme permissiveness were illustrated in psychologist Kurt Lewin's classic 1939 study of three groups of boys in after-school hobby clubs. In one group (the "democratic" group), the adult provided activities and guidance, but encouraged the boys to share in the decision making. In the second ("authoritarian") group, an adult gave the boys explicit instructions for every activity, and in the final ("laissez-faire") group the boys were allowed to work however they pleased, with minimal supervision.

The boys were then observed with and without grown-ups present. While the adults were there, the democratic and authoritarian groups were equally productive, but the laissez-faire group accomplished little. The difference between the first two groups emerged when the adults left the room. The productivity of the "authoritarian" group (whose leader had previously dictated all their activity) dropped sharply, but the kids in the "democratic" group (who'd been given choices within a clear set of guidelines) kept working, unaffected by the absence of their leader.[9]

How can you provide your child some choice within the kind of structure that Lewin's study showed is necessary? Here's how one mother did just that to settle an ongoing struggle over school night bedtime: "As long as you can get up on your own when the alarm goes off, and be ready for school on time without reminders, you can choose a bedtime between eight and nine o'clock," Marilyn told her son Tommy. "If I have to get you up in the morning, though, I'll choose your bedtime the next night."

Notice that Marilyn determined the range of choice (between 8 P.M. and 9 P.M.), as well as the criteria for success (if she has to wake Tommy up, he'll lose his option to choose). But Tommy had some sayso. A few months later, after Tommy showed that he could make responsible decisions, Marilyn also let him decide what time to get up in the morning (as long as he was ready for school on time).

AD HOC RULES

In addition to standing principles like getting to school on time and doing homework, you'll occasionally want to devise an ad hoc rule.

For example, when psychologist Ed Lonky's daughter was nine, she loved R. L. Stein's scary books so much she hardly read anything else. One day Lonky and his wife told Megan she had to choose a nonfiction book for her next book report, explaining that it would help develop her interests, and that reading nonfiction is a good way to learn new things. "What's something you'd like to know more about?" they asked their daughter, who mentioned horses and their whale watch trip the previous summer on Cape Cod. Megan ended up choosing a book about Jacques Cousteau. "You don't only say 'you have to,'" Lonky explains. "You also explain the reason."[10]

When you step in with a new limit, explain why. Explanations seemed to help when I made ad hoc rules for my son Zach. For example, he often resisted making time schedules for his work, preferring to fly (academically speaking) by the seat of his pants. When he repeatedly neglected "making a plan" for researching and writing a long report, I made a free time activity conditional on his making his plan or finishing a major assignment: "Before you can go skateboarding with your friends, you need to make a schedule for getting your social studies report done. If you don't make a plan you could end up doing it all at the last minute, and you won't have time to revise and polish it."

Make your "ad hoc" rules very sparingly, though. If you step in often, your child will end up feeling too controlled.

RELIEF FROM BATTLE FATIGUE: SETTING UP A HOMEWORK ROUTINE

You can use this same method of "choice within a framework" to set up a homework routine with your child.

Start by making as few rules as possible—only those you must make. You might, for example, only say, "Homework must be completed every night."

If this rule alone is insufficient, create some additional constraints. But offer choices like these:

- Shall homework be started before dinner?
- Should homework be finished before the TV goes on?
- Can it be interrupted with phone calls?
- Is it okay to do homework in front of the TV? with the radio on?

If you work these rules out with your child, rather than handing them down from on high, she'll know them ahead of time and she'll be more likely to accept them as fair. You may want to write agreed-upon rules into a contract that each of you signs. If you disagree with your child's choice, see if you can agree on a test period.

For example, if your child wants to do homework in front of the television, you might agree to let him do it for a week or two to demonstrate he can do it satisfactorily (which you can judge by seeing whether he keeps his grades up or by checking with his teacher) with background television. If he fails this test, unplug the tube.

Your child will also feel like she has a voice if you let her choose (within your limits) the consequences for breaking rules. Ask her questions like these:

- "What do you think should happen if you don't finish your homework once?"
- "What should happen if you're not able to get it done several days in a row?"
- "Can we agree that if your grades don't improve on the next report card we'll change our homework policy?"

Consequences should flow from the broken rule. If your daughter doesn't finish her homework, requiring her to start it earlier the next day is better than moving up her bedtime or taking away her dessert.

Make sure you follow through on your policy. The rules shouldn't be up for renegotiation every day, although you'll make rare exceptions for a special occasion or emergency.

Include *your* responsibilities in the agreement too. Here's a contract Jon and his dad created and posted on the refrigerator:

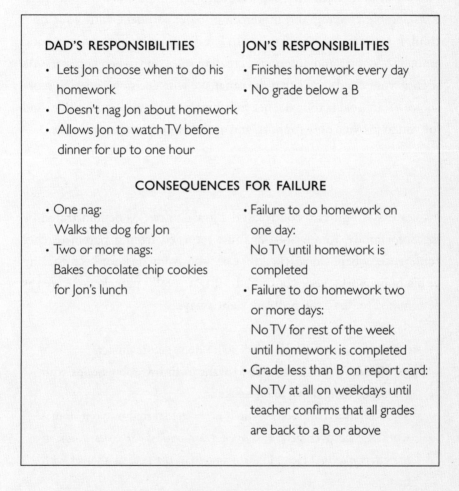

DAD'S RESPONSIBILITIES

- Lets Jon choose when to do his homework
- Doesn't nag Jon about homework
- Allows Jon to watch TV before dinner for up to one hour

JON'S RESPONSIBILITIES

- Finishes homework every day
- No grade below a B

CONSEQUENCES FOR FAILURE

- One nag:
  Walks the dog for Jon
- Two or more nags:
  Bakes chocolate chip cookies for Jon's lunch

- Failure to do homework on one day:
  No TV until homework is completed
- Failure to do homework two or more days:
  No TV for rest of the week until homework is completed
- Grade less than B on report card:
  No TV at all on weekdays until teacher confirms that all grades are back to a B or above

As your child gets older, her decision-making ability will improve, and you should give her increasing amounts of choice. In the first through third or fourth grades, you may need to help your child keep track of assignments and supervise her fairly closely. By the fifth or sixth grade, however, children should be able to organize and finish their homework assignments without you having to impose rules, although they may need help working out plans for long-term projects.

But age is not always the best predictor of children's ability to handle responsibility. Younger children are often eager to do their schoolwork and need little supervision, while some older children need considerable coaxing and monitoring. So experiment with your own child. If you aren't sure what he can handle, start by giving him a good amount of choice and autonomy, creating rules only when necessary. As soon as your child shows that she can make wise decisions, give her more choice. Your goal is to make her fully autonomous and responsible, and for you to provide only support, and as little monitoring as possible.

Resist Taking Over

It's not easy to give up control and allow choices, as demonstrated by the Soto family. Karen Soto has just returned from a parent-teacher conference, where she learned that her son Andy has not been turning in his homework. Very concerned—if not totally panicked—Karen is determined to "fix" the problem right away:

MOM: Let's start your homework so it's done before dinner.

ANDY: I'll do it in a little while. I want to throw a few hoops with Cory. I'm going down to his house.

MOM: No basketball today—you'll never get started on your homework. Come over here and open your books. *(She sits down at the kitchen table.)* Here, I'll help you do it. Let's get math over with first.

ANDY *(reluctantly)*: I hate math. I'm gonna do that last.

MOM: All the more reason to get it out of the way. Let's get going. I'll give you some cookies when we finish. Hand me your math book and your assignment sheet and let's see what we need to do.

ANDY: Aw, c'mon Mom, let me do it later. *(Spinning his basketball impatiently, and edging toward the door.)* I just got home from school! Cory's waiting for me.

MOM: This is more important. You've got to start doing better on your homework or you'll have a bad report card, and if you have a bad report card you'll have to go to summer school and if you don't pass summer school you'll flunk fifth grade and you'll never grow up to be a doctor. You know, your cousins do *their* homework right when they get home from school.

Andy sits down with his mother glumly, bouncing his basketball on the floor and looking everywhere but at the books and papers his mother has laid out on the kitchen table. Notice that Andy doesn't make a single choice; his mother is in control. On this day Andy (or, more precisely, Andy and his mother) will complete the homework. And if Karen continues to keep such a tight grip on Andy's homework, by year-end she'll be very competent in the fifth-grade curriculum. Andy, on the other hand, will have learned little and improved his sense of responsibility even less.

Here's how one dad allowed some choice without budging from the basic rule that homework must be done:

DAD: When do you plan to do your homework?

JONATHAN: I did some of it at Boys' Club after school.

DAD: How about the rest? Can you do it before dinner?

JONATHAN: But I want to try out the video game Josh lent me. I have to give it back to him tomorrow.

DAD: Well, how about doing the homework right after dinner then?

JONATHAN: But there's two shows I want to see on TV. I'll do it right after them.

DAD: Too risky. Homework is important, and by the time you watch two shows, you'll be tired. You'll have to choose between the video game now and TV after dinner, because I don't see time for both.

Let Your Child Choose His Work Style

My daughter likes to do her homework on the floor, and my son likes to do it in the family room. Your child may prefer the sofa, or even—a desk! Some kids like frequent short breaks, others like one long break in the middle of homework. While one child likes to munch while he studies, another might not. Most of these approaches make no difference, and letting your child dictate them will give her a healthy sense of control.

Once I walked into a second- and third-grade classroom at UES and found kids curled up under tables, sitting on the steps, lying on the floor and leaning against the piano—everywhere but sitting in chairs. Some were clutching stuffed animals; others had taken their shoes off. All I could hear was the sound of pages turning while these children read books chosen from a small array provided by the teacher. "It's silent reading time," the teacher whispered to me. Noticing my perplexed expression, she added, "Oh, the kids like to find their special places and get comfortable when they read. I let them do it because it gives them a sense of control. And they've learned to manage the freedom pretty well. I almost never have to tell them to stop talking."

Don't Hover

Once your child is working on his own, keep a little distance. Don't pressure him by looking over his shoulder while he works or continually asking him how it's going. Some kids like their parents nearby, and others don't. Be sensitive to your child's preferences. For most kids, the best strategy is simply to be available to help when asked. If you can't be there and your child needs help, try to enlist a grandparent, neighbor, or an older brother or sister to take your place.

Don't Use Guilt or Obligation

Have words like these ever sprung to your lips?

- "We're paying thousands of dollars to that parochial school (that private school/for this house in a good school district) so you can get a good education. What reward do we get for that? You don't even study!"
- "Your mother and I put money away every week to pay for your college education and we haven't taken a vacation in the last ten years. The least you can do is put a little effort into your schoolwork."

Comments such as these imply that your child should study for your sake, not his. So avoid guilt tripping. However valid your reasoning, your child won't buy it and it will only make him feel controlled.

Using the Language of Autonomy

It's amazing how phrasing the same comment differently can radically alter the listener's feelings. Promoting feelings of autonomy is often simply a question of using language that makes it clear your child has a choice.

Studies have shown, for example, that subtle differences in giving directions affect whether people feel in control or controlled and, consequently, how well they perform. For example, psychologist Ann Boggiano and her colleagues gave thirty-four college students a set of analytical reasoning problems from the information booklet of a standardized test, the Graduate Record Examination (GRE). All the students were taught the same strategy for solving the problems. Next the experimenters told half the students they "should" use that strategy. The other half, who were told to work any way they chose, solved more problems than the first group. Why? Their greater sense of self-determination, Boggiano believed, allowed them to think in a "more flexible, less rigid manner" and concentrate more intensely on the task at hand.[11]

Similarly, you can imply that your child has a choice if, instead of issuing orders you ask him questions, use "empowering language," and give information as described below.[12]

ASK QUESTIONS

- To remind your child of his responsibilities: "Do you have any math homework tonight?" "Would you like to read your chapter book at the library while I look up the car ratings in *Consumer Reports*?" "Do you think you could finish studying your spelling words by the time I finish the dishes? Would you like me to quiz you on them then?"
- To jump-start your child's planning: "How many days do you think it will take you to finish your math packet?" "Do you think you'll have enough time to finish writing your poem if you start at 6:30?" "If you went to the basketball game tonight, when would you do your homework?"
- To secure a commitment: "Would you agree to turning off the television every night at 7 P.M.?" "Are you willing to try to bring that grade up to a B?" "What about going to summer school for six weeks, and sports camp for four weeks?"

USE EMPOWERING LANGUAGE

When you make suggestions, show that you recognize your child is in charge of her own learning: "I haven't even started cooking yet, so you have time before dinner to get started on your homework." "You may want to participate in the geography decathlon next year." "If you really want to qualify for the concert orchestra next year, you might want to set up a practice schedule starting now." "You may want to think about doing your homework Saturday so you won't have to stay up late after your scout hike on Sunday."

PROVIDE INFORMATION

A neutral statement of fact can give your child a hint, without your telling her what to do:

- "Last time you wrote a report you did a paragraph every night. How did that work out for you?"
- "I like to use a thesaurus to avoid repeating the same words."
- "One way to learn how to draw is to copy from the Old Masters."
- "When Bill Bradley wanted to become a great basketball player, he practiced a thousand foul shots every afternoon."

Last night I was driving while a friend gave me directions. Instead of "Get over to the left lane," she said, "The left lane goes toward Pasadena." It may seem like a trivial difference, but I realized I didn't feel pressured or controlled when she put it that way.

Choosing After-School and Weekend Activities

Unless your family has strong traditions (like religious school) that require your child's participation, choosing her after-school or weekend activities can give your child some real control over her life. So put away your own desires to recapture the pleasures of your childhood or make up for your own mistakes. Within your budget and time limits, let your child try different activities and choose which one to pursue. Whether it's scouting, soccer, ballet lessons, computer classes, or karate, your child will be more energetic and enthusiastic (and reap more benefit) if she's allowed to choose her own activities.

When Meredith was in elementary school I hired a piano teacher. Meredith didn't seem to mind at first, although she rarely practiced. I tried hard not to pressure her, but I must have conveyed in a thousand ways that I really wanted her to carry on the family tradition of being a good pianist. After about a year of lessons (only weeks after I'd bought a new piano) Meredith blurted out that she was taking piano only to please me. She really didn't like it, she said. I told her that when she grew up she'd regret not sticking with piano. I even enlisted several of my friends to tell her how much they regretted abandoning music lessons as children. But the more I tried to persuade her, the more Meredith resisted, so I gave up. A few years later Meredith asked to start up piano lessons again. This time I was careful to be supportive rather than coercive. "Well, if you really want to," I said. "I guess so . . ." Now Meredith claims to love piano (although she still doesn't practice much).

Don't subvert your child's autonomy by telling him which choice you want him to make. But you can supply information. ("Swimming is fun and you get to build up your strength and race a lot." "Clarinet is neat because eventually you play in an orchestra.") And you can certainly give your opinion, if your child asks for it.

If your child doesn't have enough information to make a choice, you might specify a length of time for him to try the activity (unless he's really dead set against it). Then allow him to choose. For example, my friend Amy had her son play baseball for one season, but let him choose whether to play the second year (he decided not to).

Once she's chosen an activity, don't limit your child's choices unnecessarily within it. If your son takes drawing lessons, don't tell him what to draw (and certainly not what color to make the bear's tongue). If your daughter wants to delay going on toe shoes another six months, let her. Leaving such decisions to your child will fuel rather than smother her enthusiasm by promoting her feelings of self-determination.

Life is full of opposites, and autonomy and closeness are one such dueling pair. A sense of autonomy is a critical component of your child's self-motivation, but a close relationship with you is just as important. Let's look next at how to promote your child's love of learning by ensuring a close, secure relationship.

6

The Power of Your
Caring Connection

"What a drag," grumbles ten-year-old Larry, bursting into the kitchen and slinging his backpack to the floor. "I can't believe I have all this homework! Why does my teacher pile it on like this when she knows we all want to watch the basketball playoffs tonight!"

"Oh come on, you can't have that much," says Dad, absentmindedly thumbing through the sports section.

His mother adds, "Larry, you got three Cs on your last report card, and your father and I are not going to stand for that. You better get to work now, because we expect to see some big improvements."

Larry looks down at the floor miserably, trudges to his room and flops on his bed, sliding CD headphones on his ears and turning up the volume.[1]

Larry's parents have the best of intentions. His dad figures that making light of Larry's homework will help his son feel less pressured, and his mom wants Larry to take responsibility for his grades. Unfortunately, his parents are succeeding only in making Larry feel that they don't understand at all what he's going through. Yet making your child feel understood and supported is key to the kind of close parent-child relationship that promotes children's self-motivation to learn.

University of Rochester psychologist Richard Ryan and two colleagues demonstrated the crucial role of parent-child relationships in a 1994 study of students in a Rochester, New York, public school. They surveyed 318 boys and 288 girls about their relationships to their parents and their attitude toward schoolwork. The researchers found that the closer the students felt to their parents—the more they thought they could rely on and confide in them—the more self-motivated they were academically.[2] Another study of 456 kids in grades three to six found that the more kids believed their parents were interested in their lives and supported them, the more competent the kids felt, and the higher their academic achievement.[3]

Three Ingredients of Your Relationship

Close parent-child relationships, say researchers, have three interrelated ingredients:

Acceptance: Your child knows you love him unconditionally.
Connection: You're warmly interested and involved in your child's life, sensitive and responsive to her needs.
Support: You respect your child for who she is, and support her growing autonomy.

How does this kind of close, caring relationship promote your child's motivation to learn? There are four ways.

The first concerns the emotional security created by a solid parent-child relationship. Motivation researchers examining the effect of kids' relationships on their learning began with the British child psychiatrist John Bowlby's assertion that people are most effective when they have at least one trusted person "standing behind them"—what psychologists refer to as a "secure attachment." In one experiment Ann Frodi and her colleagues examined the value of a secure relationship by testing the attachment of forty-one one-year-olds to their mothers. Thirty-one of the babies were found to be "securely attached"—for example, they were not seriously distressed when their mothers left the room—and the other ten less so. The researchers then gave the babies toys, such as Busy Boxes and Shape Sorters. The thirty-one securely attached children played more persistently and more competently with the toys than the children with weaker attachments. They were also more curious and venturesome.[4]

Parents' support "contributes to a child's inner security," explain Richard Ryan and his colleague Jessica Solky, "which is in turn reflected in the child's ability and willingness to be a curious investigator of the surrounding world.[5]

Like a gymnast's spotter or a high-wire acrobat's safety net, the secure base of support you give your child allows her to take on the challenges that are essential to learning; she knows you'll be there for her whether she succeeds or fails. (You may have noticed a similar phenomenon in your work—when your job is secure, aren't you more willing to take on a risk or challenge?)

Second, a trusting relationship with your child gives you credibility. It is the oil that allows the machinery of self-motivated learning to run smoothly. For example, when you tell your child she's competent or assure her, "You can do it!" her trust means she will believe you. Likewise, your child is more likely to discuss rules and frameworks with good will (chapter 5) when he believes you really have his best interests at heart.

Third, a close relationship clues you in to your child's life. It allows him to be open and honest about what he's doing, thinking, and feeling—to tell you when he is happy and thriving, or when he is worried or needs help. The more easily your communication flows, the better you can follow your child's progress, point out his competencies, offer help when needed, and judge when to increase his autonomy.

Finally, if your relationship is one of mutual respect, your child will "internalize" or adopt your values, including your belief that working hard and doing well in school are important. She is more likely to emulate your enthusiasm. And she will want to achieve the expectations you have for her—not because she fears punishment, but because she has adopted them as her own.

So what can you do to ensure this kind of close relationship with your child?

ACCEPTANCE: SHOWING YOU CARE, NO MATTER WHAT

Richard Ryan once had a girl in his private practice whose parents made her feel that if she didn't do well in school, she was no good. "Jennifer got worse and worse in school," remembers the psychologist. "It was like she was saying to her parents, 'Look, I want you to love me and if you're only going to love me for doing well, I'm going to push against it.'"[6]

It's fine to let your child know that grades are important, but it's harmful if she thinks you base your love for her on grades. That sets your child up for two choices: she can try in school with the fear of losing your love hovering above her like a black cloud. Or she can become so anxious that, like Jennifer, she stops studying altogether. Kids should feel secure in your love, no matter what. That means accepting them as they are, not for "being good" or for an all-A report card. My friend Noreen puts it this way: "I tell Vincent and Juliet they can tell me anything, no matter how good or bad it is," she says. "I say, 'It won't change the way I feel. I'll still love you.' I don't think kids can hear that enough." "When they do tell me things I don't approve of," she adds, "I try to hold back my anxiety or anger and explain to them, in as caring and accepting a voice as I can muster, why they're doing something harmful or wrong."

So make sure to tell your child you care for him. Don't assume he already knows your feelings, or that buying him the latest computer game or the spiffiest soccer gear will do the trick. Despite the claims of Madison Avenue and of whiny kids, "things" don't convey your love. Hugs and affectionate words will.

Don't contradict your loving words by making your child feel bad or worthless when you're angry or frustrated. If you have to let off steam, take the dog for a walk or knead some bread dough. And however quickly they jump into your mind, avoid hurtful remarks like these:

- "I give up. I've done everything I can, and you won't even meet me halfway."
- "Why can't you be like your sister? She does her homework without even being reminded."
- "Okay, flunk the fifth grade if you want. I don't even care anymore."
- "If you really cared about Dad and me, you'd put out some effort."

Gestures Show You Care

The little things you do matter a great deal. When Meredith, who is still in high school, has a test or singing tryouts, I make her French toast with canned peaches for breakfast. When I pick her up after swim practice, I bring her a snack because I know she'll be famished. When she comes home from school sick and doesn't want to be left alone, I bring my work into her room to be close by.

It is difficult for stressed-out working parents to look for more to do. But it's amazing how powerful a small gesture can be to a child. These little expressions of love and affection take only a bit of thought and a few minutes, but they mean far more than a trip to Disneyland.

Think about what makes your heart soar. It's not the expensive perfume your child buys for you with his father's help. It's the burnt toast he brings to your bed when you aren't feeling well, or the crayon picture he draws to decorate your office. Just as these small offerings make you feel treasured, your little gestures will make your child feel nurtured and loved.

CONNECTING: TO KNOW YOUR CHILD
IS TO UNDERSTAND HIM

Making sure your child knows you are interested in him and making him feel understood are at the root of a flourishing parent-child relationship. Indeed, research has shown decisively that children whose parents are attuned to their needs and feelings tend to be more curious, to take more initiative in school, and to learn better.[7]

When your child is a baby, taking care of her is relatively simple. By holding, feeding, and diapering her, you let her know you understand every gurgle, whine, and wail. When she smiles, you smile back. When she's upset, you hold her close and sing softly. When she makes noises, you talk back as if she understands, instinctively nourishing her developing language. You meet your baby's every need, and she responds with her attachment and trust.

But tuning in to your toddler or school-age child's needs is more complex and often demands some conscious effort on your part. Here are some ways to stay involved in your child's life and keep your connection strong:

Take an Interest in Her Daily Life

As your child enters day care, preschool, or school, taking an interest in his life means knowing what happened when you were apart. Some kids spill everything at the slightest prompting, but others need questions more specific than "How was school today?" or "What's new?" Try questions like these:

- Toddlers and preschoolers: "What did you do when you played outside today?" "Did Mrs. Rosen read you a story today? What was it about?" "What is your job in the classroom this week?" "Did anything happen in the dress-up corner today?"

- School-age kids: "What was the most interesting (enjoyable, fun, exciting) thing you learned today?" "What did you learn in social studies (math, reading, music) today?" "Was Amanda nicer today?" "Who won the lunchtime soccer tournament?"

Ask your child for a guided tour of the classroom one day after school. Seeing what she's doing and what interests her will give you lots of ideas for questions later on, like "How is the white rat in your classroom doing?" "Did you work in the class garden today? Has anything sprouted yet?"

Don't forget to listen attentively to your child's answers.

Spend Time Together

Spending time together—whether hanging out in the backyard, shooting hoops in the driveway, or baking a cake—will always be crucial to your relationship. (Even if your preteen pretends she doesn't recognize you at the mall, she still wants to spend time with you. Trust me.) Most kids love it when you create family rituals like ice skating every Christmas Eve, going to a movie together on Friday nights, or playing board games on Saturday mornings. (Watching TV together doesn't count, unless you're discussing it or cheering for a team together.)

I was often preoccupied with my work when I drove Meredith home from elementary school. I tried to sound attentive by muttering "hmm" and "uh huh" as she told me about her day. One afternoon when she was six, she stopped in the middle of a sentence, folded her arms, and cried out, "Mom, I know you're not listening to me. PAY ATTENTION!" I am lucky to have a daughter who demands what she needs from me. Many other children just stop talking.

If time is precious, use well the time you have. Have a conversation in the car; talk or play with one child while you wait for another to finish sports or music practice; chat with your child while you cruise the grocery store together or stand in line at the bank. The older your child gets, the more you can share your life with her, which will encourage her to do the same with you.

If you and your child are often at odds, spending recreational time together is all the more critical. Some amount of conflict is inevitable between every parent and child, but don't let it color your entire relationship. If fighting is pushing you apart, make a special effort to spend pleasant, conflict-free time together. It will probably mean holding back criticisms and rebukes, even when they seem to be called for. Reassure yourself as you bite your tongue that building a positive, caring relationship will, in the long run, render your advice and opinions more effective.

Make Your Child Feel Understood

Remember misunderstood Larry? His mom and dad just finished a parenting course at their local community center. Let's rewind the video and watch them now: Larry bursts into the kitchen complaining. "What a drag! I can't believe I have all this homework!" His dad sympathizes. "What a bummer! Your teacher does seem to give you a lot more homework than your sister had in fifth grade."

"What time do the playoffs start?" his mom asks. "Seven," says Larry, looking up at the clock, which already reads 5:30. "It sounds like you have a lot to do," says his mom, chopping an onion. "But if you start right away, could you finish your homework before the playoffs begin? We could have dinner a little late. In fact, if you finish your homework I'm willing to make an exception and let you eat dinner while you watch the playoffs. Your dad may even want to join you."

Larry's face suddenly brightens. His parents haven't let him off the homework hook, but they understand how important the playoffs are to him, and will even make it possible for him to watch the game tonight.

Larry's mother respected his love of basketball by offering a compromise in the family routine. His father showed he understood Larry by using a technique called mirroring, developed by psychologists to help make children feel understood.

Mirroring and Other Tactics That Get Kids Talking

Mirroring means listening carefully to your child and reflecting back her thoughts and feelings—repeating her words exactly or rephrasing them. Here's an example:

> MOM: How was school today?
>
> JULIE *(almost in tears)*: It was awful! I did horrible on my math test.
>
> MOM: You did horribly?
>
> JULIE: Yeah, I got all messed up when I had to borrow from the other column!
>
> MOM: Oh, you got confused . . .
>
> JULIE: I mean I thought I knew how to do it but the problems on the test were really different from the homework.
>
> MOM: I see—you knew what to do when you did your homework, but then you couldn't do it on the test?

By mirroring Julie's words, her mother makes her feel understood and draws her out. There are other ways to encourage your child to share. For example, if your child is enthusiastic, reflect and share her enthusiasm: "That's wonderful!" If something sad has happened, reflect that too: "I'm so sorry." "Oh, that *is* a shame."

If she stalls in mid-story, ask her, "What happened next?" or "Then what did he say?" You can also share a similar experience and say how it made you feel.

Beware of common conversation stoppers, like

- Blurting out your own feelings: "I don't think I can take any more disasters today." (Sometimes said with hands over ears.)
- I-told-you-so's: "See what happens when you put your homework off till the last minute! I warned you you'd get a bad grade."
- Trying to force your child to think or feel a certain way: "You've got to realize that reading is the most important subject."
- Giving unsolicited advice or opinions: "If I were you I'd do the math first, since it's the easiest for you." "You'd do better on the test if you started studying farther ahead of time."

You needn't *approve* of everything your child tells you. "A lot of people who want to feel connected to their child think the main thing one does is say nice things or be positive or reassuring," says Richard Ryan. "That's not really the key issue. The key issue is making them feel that you are interested in and able to understand their point of view."[8] Your understanding will relax them, and they'll keep talking.

Emotional Coaching

Emotional coaching is another effective way to make your child feel understood.[9] It will also build your child's self-understanding. Your role as "emotion coach" includes helping your child put words or labels on her feelings. You are also validating her emotions—showing her that they are normal and okay.

Here's how one dad practiced emotional coaching:

JULIAN: Aw geez, I can't believe what happened today.

DAD: You really seem upset. What happened?

JULIAN: I forgot to study the second math worksheet, and l missed half the problems in the test.

DAD: I can see why you feel frustrated.

JULIAN: Well, I'm more like, mad at myself.

DAD: I know what you mean. *(Chuckles.)* You know what I did once? I worked really hard on an English essay, but the day it was due I left it at home. After I got home I rode my bike back to school. The teacher wasn't there so I left it on her desk. She still dropped my grade for lateness. I felt so stupid.

Notice that Dad avoids the traps parents commonly fall into when faced with a child's negative emotions. He doesn't

- Deny them: "Oh come on, you can't really feel bad about that."
- Try to persuade him to give them up: "You just have to forget about it, and move on."
- Soothe him: "Well, but you wrote such a nice poem yesterday! The math test is no big deal. Don't let it bother you."
- Express anger or impatience: "I told you to make sure you'd studied everything you were supposed to. How can you be so thickheaded?"
- Try to distract: "Let's watch the Lakers game tonight together."

Even though Julian's frustration makes his dad uncomfortable (no parent wants his child to feel bad), he doesn't try to "fix" Julian's problem right away. The goal of emotional coaching is to accept your child's emotion as is. (You can help him problem-solve, if need be, later on.) Instead, Julian's dad shows that he can tolerate his son's bad feelings, and even empathize with him. This makes Julian feel understood.

Here are some tips to help you with emotional coaching:

- Ask questions: "What happened?" "What made you so happy? Angry?" "How did that (assignment, grade, award) make you feel?" "Did your teacher's comment make you feel (ashamed, excited, proud)?"
- Label your child's feelings: "You seem frustrated." "You look pretty unhappy about that." "Your face looks angry." "You sound disappointed." "I bet you felt (worried, scared, delighted, pleased, happy)."

- Empathize to let your child know you understand his emotion: "I know what you mean." "I can understand how frustrating that is!" "I understand." "I can imagine how you feel!"
- Empathize by recounting a similar experience, as Julian's father did. (Kids love to hear you've been through the same thing.) For example, you might say, "I felt frustrated when I was learning grammar too," or "I remember teachers who refused to listen to my point of view. It made me mad too."

Empathizing is especially important when you're setting limits on your child's negative behavior: "I know you're really frustrated with your homework, but you can't throw your book down the incinerator chute." "I understand that you want to go outside to play right now, it's such a beautiful day. But we agreed that you'd finish your homework first."

As you can see, I'm not recommending indulging your child's negative behavior. If she throws her math book against the wall or lashes out at her little brother, you can accept your child's feelings, but set limits on the behavior.[10]

Easier Said Than Done

Being understanding and empathetic can be very difficult. Faced with your child's failures and negative feelings, you may feel angry, annoyed, or helpless. Perhaps you blame yourself, or feel disappointed that she's not living up to your expectations. So knowing what to say can be easier than actually saying it.

It may help if you first vent your own feelings to a spouse or friend. Then when you feel calmer, you can bring the topic up again with your child. Bridget's mom, for example, was furious when Bridget complained about doing poorly on a presentation because she hadn't prepared (despite her mother's multiple reminders the night before). But her

mom stifled her "I-told-you-so" when Bridget first mentioned her failure. Later her mother returned to the subject:

MOM: You sounded upset this afternoon about not being prepared
   for your oral book report.
BRIDGET: Oh yeah, I feel so stupid.
MOM: What's making you feel stupid?
BRIDGET: I thought I could practice during gym class because of my
   sore knee, but instead of playing volleyball we had a lecture today
   on sportsmanship, and I had to listen.
MOM: Sounds like you took a risk by waiting till the last minute.

Reframing

Sometimes it's helpful to "reframe" your child's emotions, or look at
them from a different angle. Make sure, however, that you reframe without discounting her initial feelings, and that you really believe the new
viewpoint. For example, if your daughter felt embarrassed because she
was pulled out of class for special help, you might reframe the situation
this way: "I understand that you feel embarrassed leaving the classroom.
Extra lessons are good, though, because you learn more. And you get to
work with the tutor one-on-one, not in a big group. Maybe if you think
about all the benefits of tutoring, you'll feel better about it." (Don't
invent, "Only the smartest girls get pulled out for resource work.")

Reflecting on Your Own Childhood

Those who do not understand history, said the philosopher George
Santayana, are condemned to repeat it. Similarly, if you don't examine
your own parents' mistakes, you may visit them on your own children.
If you find that you tend to be dismissive, judgmental, or angry with
your child, try this exercise:[11]

- List things your parents often said to you (it's fun to do this with a friend).
- Check which of these you say to your children.
- Think how you felt when your mother or father said these things to you.
- Decide on a saying you'd like to change. Think up a substitute, and practice it on your spouse or a friend.

Be Positive

Psychologists have an unfortunate tendency to focus on negative feelings, which give them an opportunity to solve problems. As a result, they sometimes neglect the positive.

That doesn't mean you can't, like Desmond's mother, label positive emotions and share in your child's happiness, pride, satisfaction, and other positive good feelings:

DESMOND: Mom, guess what! I got elected to student council!

MOM: Oh, I can see how excited you are! But I'm not surprised. That speech you practiced was dynamite. You must be very proud of yourself!

DESMOND: Yeah, I guess I do feel proud.

MOM: What did you think when you found out you'd won?

DESMOND: I was really excited. All the kids clapped, and Chris gave me a high five and my teacher said, "Congratulations!"

MOM: *(laughs happily)*

When Your Connection Needs Repairing

One afternoon when Zach was six I picked him up at the school he attended before UES. "I hate music class!" he cried. "Miss Shepherd is mean!"

"Oh Zach, this was just the first time you've had music," I said. "Miss Shepherd is nice."

Zach's lip jutted out in a pout and he sunk down into his seat. When I asked him how his team had done in the lunchtime basketball tournament, he just grunted.

If you've been dismissive (as I was) or have disrupted your connection with other no-nos, remember that your relationship with your child is reparable. Children are very flexible. Just like adults, they love people to listen and understand them. If you change your tune, they'll almost always respond in a flash. (Later that night, I asked Zach why he didn't like his music teacher, and he told me she had lost her temper and threatened to make his class observe ten minutes of silence if they didn't settle down. "Oh, I see why you don't like her!" I said. "That must have been scary when she lost her temper.")

Try this: ask your clammed-up child a question, and when she answers, listen attentively. Ask a question or two, again in a supportive or at least neutral tone. Hold back any judgmental thoughts such as "Geez, I told you not to hang around with those boys. They're nothing but trouble." Avoid anxious questions: "You mean you think you might flunk another science test?" Follow up the next day with a few mirroring conversations and a dash of empathy. Let your child know you're his most interested listener and whenever possible, the most approving and affectionate as well.

Now that we've seen how your unconditional love and your interest and involvement in your child's life build the kind of relationship that promotes self-motivation in your child, let's move on to the third ingredient of a close relationship: support for your child's autonomy.

SUPPORT: RESPECTING YOUR CHILD FOR WHO HE IS

When the Nobel Prize–winning UCLA pharmacology professor Louis Ignarro was growing up, his parents bought him six chemistry sets, each more sophisticated than the last. His father also helped him make

HOW ONE MOTHER REPAIRED A
COMMUNICATION BREAK WITH HER SON

"When Mark turned ten, he suddenly stopped talking to me about his friends and what they did together, and even about school and baseball," my friend Carole told me. "I felt suddenly cut off from him, and kind of sad. I was really worried. Did that mean he was starting to do things he knew I'd disapprove of?

"One day in the dentist's waiting room I came across a magazine article called 'Communicating with Your Kids.' I decided to try out the article's advice—not to use Mark's comments as a springboard for telling him what he should do, and to stop greeting his enthusiasm for skateboarding with his buddies with anxious warnings about his safety.

"As I drove Mark to school every morning, I started asking him neutral questions, simply listening to his answers. Occasionally I made empathetic comments like 'That must have been frustrating.' Sometimes I told stories about similar experiences I'd had. ('Yeah, once I had a teacher like that. She liked a small group of kids in her class, and she didn't care about the others.') It took a while, but slowly Mark started confiding in me again. After a few weeks he was telling me more—of course, not all—about his life. Today our relationship is warm and close again."

rocket fuel and send up rockets. "He believed that such a kid who could create the material for bombs and rocket fuel should be allowed to continue his pursuit of chemistry," says Ignarro. However, when as a teenager Ignarro started taking apart and reassembling cars to race them, his father was disturbed. In fact, when his son brought home his first auto-racing trophy, Ignarro's father scowled, complaining that racing and fixing up car engines was a very expensive proposition. Louis Ignarro explains, "He would never come to see me race my car."

One day, however, after he'd won several races, Ignarro came home from school to find that his father had built him a trophy case. "He had a change of heart," remembers the Nobel Prize winner, "because he recognized the talents that I had developed."

"He said, 'I'm proud of you, son, but please don't ruin the cars.'"[12]

It took a little time, but ultimately Ignarro's dad respected who he was and even supported an interest that cut against his own grain. In a similar way, your interest and involvement in your child's life will clarify the ways he's separate and different from you. You'll know who he really is and what his goals are. That will put you in the best position to help him, as the Mamas and Papas song says, "go where he wants to go, do what he wants to do." In other words, by supporting the autonomy I talked about in chapter 5, you'll help your child blaze her own path and be herself.

Once you understand your child's perspective, sometimes you'll want to show that you support it with your actions. If nothing comes to mind, volunteer with words that make it clear you're on your child's side, like "How can I help you?" "Is there anything you'd like me to do?"

Don't worry that supporting your child's growing autonomy will drive you apart. As he grows, your child needs less help pouring his breakfast cereal and more with his homework, less help bandaging her knees and more help deciding which soccer cleats fit. Your close connection will also clue you in to these changes in your child's needs, which in turn will intensify her feelings that you are on her side and have her best interests at heart.

The more you support your child's autonomy, the more self-reliant she'll become, but that needn't sever your emotional connection. Even when she grows up, leaves home, and takes care of herself, your emotional connection will remain.

Don't worry either that your assistance will smother your child or make him feel angry. He'll feel that way if you are controlling. But if you support who he is and what he wants, your help will feel nurturing.[13] It will contribute to the positive, secure relationship he needs to take risks and pursue the learning that he most loves.

Adopting Your Values

Every day when Kara Simon gets home from school, she eats an apple and some cookies, plays with her cat, Honeybun, then sits down at her desk and does her homework. Whether or not she likes what she's doing, Kara always finishes her work on time. Her mother never has to remind her to start or check to see that it's done.

Kara's fifth-grade homework is fairly traditional—a few pages of math problems, a chapter in her social studies book with questions to answer at the end, and thirty minutes on an assigned reading text. Once a week she writes a paper on a topic chosen by the teacher, and every two months she does a book report. If you ask Kara whether she enjoys school, she says, "Oh yes! I have lots of friends! And my teacher is nice, and the work is pretty easy." If you ask her whether she enjoys her homework, she would look at you with a puzzled expression. "Of course not," she'd probably answer. "It's just what you have to do."

Kara is an example of a self-motivated student who doesn't necessarily love or even enjoy learning, at least not the learning she does at school. She's conscientious and content, if not exhilarated or joyful. Certainly, many parents would settle happily for a daughter who is such a conscientious worker.

It is not realistic to expect children to love the dull, repetitive tasks they sometimes get in school. But as Kara points out, they have to do it to succeed. One of the benefits of a positive relationship with your child is that it helps you convince him that he should be conscientious and responsible and that doing well in school is important, so he'll want to plow through homework, even when it's boring.

Like Kara, we all have values that make us do willingly things that we don't particularly enjoy. You might, for example, read the newspaper every day because you believe you have a responsibility to be an informed citizen. Perhaps you took a foreign language because you valued relating to people from other countries in their own language. These activities have a practical use, but they also reflect your values— your beliefs about what it takes to be a good person.

Similarly, cherishing education and doing well in school aren't inborn; nor are the values of being hardworking and responsible. Children have to learn these values from their parents and other significant people in their lives, a process psychologists refer to as "internalization."

This "internalization" process is necessary for every self-motivated student, because while you can make learning fun at home, you have little control over the work your child receives at school. Many schools assign a great deal of boring work, and even the best teachers sometimes give tedious assignments. It helps your child to know she's competent and can succeed, but to do work that's not appealing, she also needs to internalize your belief that schoolwork is extremely important and worth doing no matter what. *Every* student needs to have adopted these values as his own to motivate him at least some of the time.

While your ultimate aim may be a child who loves learning, having one who studies "because that's what you're supposed to do" is not to be sneezed at. The efforts of many fine students are fueled mainly by their internalized value of doing a good job in school. Such motivation may fall short of learning for the pure pleasure of it, but since values are internal to your child, your child experiences a feeling of autonomy—of doing something because *she* wants to, not because someone else tells her to.

HOW KIDS ADOPT OUR VALUES

Parents begin to transmit the value of learning very early, when they praise or reward their child for exerting effort. For example, when Kara was little, her parents praised her when she set the table or worked hard on a picture or a puzzle. She learned to anticipate their reactions and would look up expectantly for her mother's smile or her father's comment after she finished a project. Her parents didn't reward her lavishly (the danger of which I'll describe in chapter 9) but instead used the smallest effective reward—usually praise.

The Simons also demonstrated the value they placed on working hard by doing so themselves. After Emily Simon puts an hour into the family finances at the kitchen table, she announces proudly that the bills are all paid up and that she's balanced the checkbook. At dinner one night, her husband, Rafael, says he'll probably be up late preparing for a meeting the next day, and asks to trade that evening's after-dinner cleanup for double duty the following night. Gradually Kara developed an internal model of her parents' self-disciplined work, and because they have a sound relationship with her and she loves them, she wants to be like them.

At first, whenever she accomplished something, Kara had an image in her mind of her parents praising her. When she was little, she would even imitate their likely reaction out loud, sometimes in pretend play with her stuffed animals: "Good girl, you picked up your toys!" she would say, or "That's great, you worked hard on your picture!" Gradually her parents' approval (or disapproval) became so firmly implanted in her thinking that she didn't even know where it came from. The pride she felt for working hard or the guilt for slacking off became her own feelings, because her parents' values had become her own. When she went to school, she became a conscientious student, because she had adopted her parents' belief in the importance of working hard, being responsible, and learning.

Let's analyze the ways parents transmit their belief in the importance of education to their children. First we'll look at one parent's sincere but misguided attempt to convince his son to do his schoolwork.

Josh comes home from school and turns on the TV. Two hours later, when his dad comes home from work, Josh is still lying on the couch, watching sitcom reruns.

"Your relaxed pose tells me you've finished your homework," his father says sarcastically. Josh ignores him.

"Josh, your mother and I have warned you we're taking you off the basketball team if you don't pull up your grades," says his dad, exasperated. "Now get moving!"

Josh gets up sulkily without looking at his father, and slips out the back door to his favorite hiding place, a treehouse deep in the backyard.

Josh's dad is trying to make Josh adopt his values by exerting pressure—threatening him with punishment. But research shows that pressuring children to adopt their parents' values usually backfires (as you might expect after reading about the importance of autonomy in chapter 5).

"One of the remarkable findings from numerous investigations of internalization is that children appear more likely . . . to fully internalize societal values and behaviors (i.e., make them their own) . . . when less rather than more pressure is applied from without," writes psychologist Wendy Grolnick and two colleagues.[14]

COMMUNICATING YOUR VALUES DIRECTLY

If you offer your child a reward or threaten a punishment to do what you value, that constitutes pressure. But if you simply tell him your ideals, she is free to adopt them or not. So telling your child directly what you value can be quite powerful. That's what Carol Jago, an English teacher at Santa Monica High School, did when her son's soccer team played a tournament that began on a Friday morning in October. In fact, she communicated her values to the entire community in her weekly *Los Angeles Times* column. Not only did she not allow James (who plays on his state team) to miss a day of school, but she told him exactly why. "School comes first," she explained. "Academics is the foundation on which your future is built."[15] (While Jago forbade or "pressured" James not to miss school, she didn't insist he adopt her reasoning.)

In a similar way, you can tell your child clearly and directly that it is important for him to try hard in school. Point out the advantages of people who do well, and talk about the problems faced by people you know who couldn't go to school, didn't apply themselves, or dropped out. Give your child reasons she'll understand at her age. The closer they are to her experience, the better.

- "Your grandparents were immigrants and weren't able to finish school because they had to work to help support the family. They were very proud of the fact that all their children earned college degrees. Going to college has meant we can lead better lives than they were able to."
- "I know you want to sleep over at Susie's tonight, but it's a school night. We've talked about how important it is to concentrate in school, and you won't be able to do that without a good night's sleep."
- "It's really important to be able to write well. If you can't communicate your ideas clearly to other people, it's almost not worth having them."
- "If you work hard, your teacher will respect you and so will the other kids, even if they don't say so."

PAY ATTENTION TO YOUR SUBTLE MESSAGES

Children take in far more than your direct statements. They are influenced just as strongly by your subtle communications.

Consider the message in Greg's parents' reactions to their son's announcement at dinner that he did very well on a book report that he had been struggling with:

"That's nice, Greg!" says his mom, shaking grated cheese on her spaghetti.

Later on, Greg mentions that he scored ten points during the lunchtime basketball game. His dad gives him a high five, grinning.

"Way to shoot, son!" his dad crows enthusiastically. "Were they outside shots or layups? Did your team win? How is your jump shot coming along? When does the tournament season start?"

What's the message Greg's parents are inadvertently sending? That academic work is sort of important—but the *real* way to win their approval is through basketball.

Compare the indirect message sent by my friend Dorothy's father, in this excerpt from her essay:

I grew up in San Francisco where, like most Chinese kids, I had two things on my mind: school and pleasing my parents. Since the best way to please my parents was to excel in school, that boiled down to my single-minded goal of being the best at all things academic.

People wonder with envy and sometimes with racial resentment why Asian kids do so well in school: "What is it with those kids?" they think.

I know that for most Chinese kids, school is like religion. For us it was the one thing that deserved faith. The more you believed in it, the more it rewarded you, an eternal source of hope and redemption. The practice required rituals as strict and elaborate as any church. We were taught always to study at a desk, sitting straight up. The room had to be library-quiet, and background music of any kind was unthinkable. (It was not until college that I broke all these rules simultaneously, studying slouched on the bed with the radio on, sometimes ingesting pizza and Coke.)

I remember my father looking for desks for us, a task so delicate and monumental that he had to bring us children along, our small bodies mimicking the acts of writing or reading so that he could gauge their fit and comfort. The desks he bought were small, their space suited for a book, a writing pad, and little elbows—that was all. My father equipped each of them with a desk lamp whose wattage he adjusted perfectly. We were taught to keep our desks uncluttered, so our eyes and attention would focus only on whatever material was atop of them, thus bestowing upon it unrivaled importance; everything else was to be stored in the drawers. When all these elements were in place, we were ready to begin our studies. I believe that buying our desks was one of the most fulfilling things my father felt he did as a parent, a task that exemplified for him the very pinnacle of parenting.[16]

Even though Dorothy's parents seldom said directly, "Learning is important," their actions had a powerful effect: two of their daughters are college professors and the third is an engineer.

Here are some other ways to let your child know your values indirectly:

- Buy school supplies gladly to the extent your budget allows. Don't complain about the time it took or the cost, even if these are issues. You don't want your child to feel guilty about imposing on you or the family finances. If school materials aren't affordable, talk to your child's teacher or the school social worker. Most schools have extra supplies they can slip a needy student.

- Make schoolwork a priority: "We can't visit Grandma tonight because it would interfere with your homework. Let's go on Saturday." "We'll come back from the mountains Sunday morning so you'll have time to get ready for school."

- Be consistent and make only rare exceptions to rules reflecting your values. Don't take your son to social or religious events or the movies at night unless he has already finished his homework and will still get enough sleep to be alert in school the next day.

- Respect your child's schoolwork needs even when you'd like her company. "I'd really like it if you came to Jennifer's softball game with me, but if you have homework to do, I understand. We'll go to the next one together."

Here are some comments that communicate values indirectly:

- "Honey, don't bother your sister now. She's doing her homework."
- "When we move, let's try to live in Springfield, because the schools there are very good."
- "I made you a healthy breakfast so you'll be able to concentrate on your schoolwork this morning."

LIVE YOUR VALUES

What you do influences your child's values as powerfully as what you say. Like Kara's parents, model your values when you draft a report at home or do volunteer work. Don't moan and groan, procrastinate, turn work in late, or do a sloppy job. If you do, you give your child license to do the same.

WHAT IF YOU DON'T HAVE TIME TO MAKE CUPCAKES FOR THE PTA BAKE SALE?

The increasingly frequent admonishment, "Parents need to be more involved in their children's schools!" evokes guilt in many a mom or dad with an inflexible work schedule. Yes, spending time at school is one of the many ways to let your child know how much you value education. If you can take a few hours off work to volunteer in your child's kindergarten classroom, go on a field trip, or attend a PTA meeting, that's great.

But if you don't have time for these activities, you can still attend parent-teacher conferences, open house or back-to-school night, and other programs at your child's school. Read the school newsletter, get to know your child's classmates, and talk to their parents. You don't need to spend a tremendous amount of time at your child's school to learn about your child and her life there, and to show her how important her education is to you.

Learning side by side sends a strong message too. Take piano lessons together, read the funnies and other parts of the newspaper to each other, or watch a news show together on TV.

Remember Josh's father? He didn't start out so well, but after a friend gave him a few suggestions, here's what he said the next time he found Josh watching TV after school:

"Josh, I know you're having a tough time getting your homework done. I remember how hard it was for me when I was your age. Look, I have some spreadsheets to go through tonight. Let's work together on the dining room table. If we get our work finished, maybe we can catch the second half of Monday night football."

The second time around, Josh's dad modeled the desired behavior, invited Josh to join him, and even built in some additional closeness with the offer of some "guy time" watching football together.

A POTENTIALLY GREATER PAYOFF

Schoolwork that kids do because they "should" can turn into something they really enjoy, since values can "jump-start" academic effort just as rewards can. As time goes on and she gains competence, your merely conscientious child may discover an interest and start to enjoy some of her work. So, for example, while Mayan culture seemed too remote to interest your daughter at first, it may become intriguing once she gets into her social studies project. Or your son may begin his math homework just to get it over with, but become so engrossed in the challenging word problems that he forgets to watch his favorite TV show. The path toward loving learning can be short or long, so don't underestimate the role in that journey of simple, everyday conscientious behavior.

Now that we've covered the three main ingredients of loving learning—competence, autonomy, and relationship—we'll look at some ideas that can heat up your child's desire to learn, or send it to the deep freeze. The first concerns our notion of intelligence. Is IQ something you're born with, or can you increase your intelligence by working hard? We'll answer that all-important question in the next chapter.

7

Your Child Can "Get Smart" If She Works Hard

It was 1957 when Mrs. Wilson, psychologist Carol Dweck's sixth-grade teacher, was convinced that children's intelligence said everything about them. She seated her pupils in order of their IQ scores, wrote each child's IQ in big black numbers next to his name in her roll book, and assigned coveted responsibilities, such as clapping the blackboard erasers or carrying the flag in assembly, according to IQ score.

Mrs. Wilson's bizarre regime filled her students with anxiety. Although Dweck's class was the top track of the sixth grade, pupils with the relatively low IQ scores felt inferior. Worried that making mistakes would show just how dumb they were, they avoided difficult work. Kids with relatively high IQ scores were rattled too. What if they did poorly on their next standardized test and the teacher found out they really *weren't* smart?[1]

As implausible as this story may seem, it is true. And although extreme, it illustrates how much weight some teachers, and some parents too, put on the notion that children are born with different intellectual ability.

Are You Born Smart, or Can You Get Smart?

Perhaps it's no accident that Dweck, now a Columbia University professor, has spent her career examining how beliefs about intelligence affect students' motivation and achievement. She and other researchers have found that believing intelligence is fixed and inborn can damage students' internal motivation to learn. Defining intelligence as a quality that can increase through effort, on the other hand, fosters students' love of learning.

You've probably wrestled at one time or another with the relative import of inborn ability and effort. Are geniuses born or made? Does talent make the soprano's voice soar, the CPA calculate so swiftly in her head, and the athlete swish a three-pointer with such ease? Or do the experience and hard work preceding the graceful performance make all the difference?

It's a fascinating question, and there is evidence on both sides. But when it comes to children's learning, the answer is that kids who believe they can "get smart" by working hard are more likely to persist until they've learned material or mastered a skill than kids who think you have to be "born smart." Students who think you can get smarter through effort also tend to relish challenges, to consider mistakes a natural part of learning, and to bounce back from failure with new strategies. And they are far more likely to enjoy learning.

On the other hand, kids who believe intelligence is fixed think there is nothing they can do to get smarter. They have no reason to work hard or to persist when the going gets tough. You can't fault their reasoning. If you don't think you have the ability to succeed, and there's nothing you can do about your ability, why keep trying?

LOOK FOR THE PLAIN HARD WORK AND EXPERIENCE BEHIND THE TINSELED CURTAIN OF TALENT

Recently my friend Leonia wrote about traveling back to her birthplace in Poland. I was stunned by her beautifully crafted story, seemingly simple but with a deep emotional impact. "Where did she get all that talent?" I wondered, thinking of my hours struggling with writing. "She's a natural," said another friend.

Then one day I asked Leonia, a psychotherapist, how she had come by her storytelling abilities. I expected her to say airily, "Oh, I don't know. It just happened." Instead, she told me she had written her Ph.D. dissertation on folktales, and for years she has attended a storytelling group, where she listens to and tells stories each week. I realized too that as a therapist, she studies emotions every day. And she confessed to me that she had slaved over her story, revising it again and again until it felt right.

Leonia may have been born with a gift for storytelling, but clearly, she has honed her skills with a lot of hard work.

"Learned Helplessness": The Problem with Emphasizing Inborn Ability

The story of research into "born-smart" and "get-smart" beliefs began in 1964, when a young graduate student named Martin Seligman arrived at the University of Pennsylvania psychology laboratory and found it in uproar. To investigate the effect of fear on behavior, researchers had put dogs in chambers and given them electric shocks. Some of the dogs had no escape route, but the others could avoid the shocks by running to the other side of the chamber. Later all the dogs were put in chambers where they could escape the shocks. But the dogs that at first hadn't been able to escape the shocks weren't behaving as expected. Instead of hotfooting it to the other side of the chamber, they lay motionless, enduring the shocks. Baffled, the researchers had halted the study.

Seligman, however, was fascinated by the dogs' passivity. Perhaps having no control over the shocks in the first chamber, he reasoned, had taught the dogs that trying to avoid them, even when they could, would be futile. In other words, the dogs had learned to be helpless.[2] Carol Dweck, then a graduate psychology student at Yale, was intrigued by the story of the passive dogs. She had been wondering why some perfectly competent kids shy away from challenges and fall apart at the first sign of failure. Could "learned helplessness" be the reason?

Dweck launched a series of experiments to test her hunch that students will act helpless if they think academic success is out of their control. In one experiment, for example, she and a colleague gave ninety-four fifth-graders a questionnaire to determine whether they thought effort (which they could control) or factors beyond their control (like luck or ability) were the main factor in school success. Although their academic skills were roughly equal, some of the students, whom she labeled "helpless," thought they had little control over whether they succeeded or failed, whereas others emphasized the role of their own effort.

Then the researchers gave the children a passage to read, followed by seven comprehension questions. If they missed any questions they were given a review booklet and a second test. However, the review booklets contained a "red herring"; near the beginning was an irrelevant paragraph, clearly written in half the booklets, but gobbledygook in the others. The researchers wanted to see how this detour into confusion affected the children.

The irrelevant but clear paragraph affected both the "helpless" and the "effort-is-what-counts" students the same; two-thirds of each group answered the seven questions correctly this time. But the gobbledygook affected the two groups of students very differently. Seventy-two percent of the "effort-counts-more" kids aced the seven questions, but only 35 percent of the "helpless" kids did so. Failure to decipher the gobbledygook had apparently spiraled a majority of the helpless students into self-doubt so strong that they couldn't bounce back to learn.[3]

In a second study Dweck directly tested the effects of children's beliefs about intelligence. First she and her colleagues gave 229 students a questionnaire to find out whether they thought people are "born smart." The students were asked how much they agreed or disagreed with statements like these:

- "You have a certain amount of intelligence, and you really can't do much to change it."
- "You can learn new things, but you can't really change your basic intelligence."
- "Your intelligence is something about you that you can't change very much."

Next the researchers compared sixth- and seventh-grade achievement scores of students who scored high versus low on this measure of "born-smart" beliefs. While the achievement scores of the "born-smart" believers (children who agreed with the statements on the questionnaire) stayed low or declined, those of the "get-smart" believers (children who mostly disagreed with the statements) had stayed high or improved from sixth to seventh grade.[4] Many of the high achievers in sixth grade who believed intelligence is fixed had become low achievers in seventh grade.

To get a glimpse into the feelings of kids with the two different beliefs about intelligence, Dweck and a colleague encouraged a group of fifth- and sixth-graders to talk out loud as they worked on difficult problems. "Born-smart" kids complained about their ability, made irrelevant statements, and felt bored and hopeless. They said things like

"I never did have a good memory."

"By the way, I'm going to inherit money soon."

"There is a talent show this weekend, and I am going to be Shirley Temple."
"I'm bored."

"Get-smart" kids, however, gave themselves instructions, concentrated on how to fix mistakes, and felt cheerful and optimistic. They said, for example,

"I should slow down and try to figure this out."
"I love a challenge."
"I've almost got it now."

Dweck and other researchers have decisively shown the tremendous value of thinking that intelligence can increase—that *anyone* can get smart and achieve success if she tries. When kids who think this way have difficulty, they don't assume it's because they're incompetent in some unchangeable way. They think they have to try a different strategy or work at it a little longer, or maybe that they lack a necessary skill. So rather than quitting when they hit a roadblock, they persist and try to figure a way over or around it.

Avoiding Helplessness: Raising a "Get-Smart" Kid

Research shows that you can change the mind of a child who thinks you have to be "born smart." Dweck showed how to do that when she worked with a group of very helpless eight- to thirteen-year-olds. Every day for a month she gave them fifteen sets of math problems to finish within a certain time limit. She rigged the sessions for half of the kids so that they *always* succeeded. The other half, however, were set up to fail two or three times in fifteen tries. Each time they failed, Dweck told the students it was because they "hadn't tried hard enough."

At the end of the month, the "success-only" kids (who you might think—unless you've read chapter 4—would have had high self-confidence) had not improved their math problem-solving abilities. But the students who had failed several times and been taught to attribute their failure to their lack of effort, now tried harder and looked for new strategies each time they failed. As a result, they increased the number of problems per minute they could solve correctly.

Even more interesting, their teachers (who didn't know which child had been in which group) told Dweck that the kids who had been taught to blame mistakes on lack of effort had improved their classroom performance noticeably. They were now more persistent, and some of them were asking for more work![5]

Dweck's technique is one of several you can use to persuade your child that she can get smarter if she works hard and persists. Let's begin this discussion by comparing the methods of two parents dealing with children weighted down by born-smart thinking:

BAD AND GOOD WAYS TO DEAL WITH
BORN-SMART BELIEFS

BRANDON: I can't figure out these math word problems.

DAD: But sweetheart, you're so smart! I know you can do it.

BRANDON: I'm not as smart as Timmy. He's a math whiz. He figured these out on the school bus.

DAD: You're just as smart as Timmy. Don't let him intimidate you. I don't care if his mother is a brain surgeon. Remember, your grandfather was mayor of Springfield and your aunt wrote a book on Japanese vases! Our family has always been brainy!

AMY: Mom, I can't figure out these math word problems.

MOM: What's getting in your way?

AMY: I don't know. I just can't do them. I'm not good at math.

MOM: How long have you been trying?

AMY: Since dinner.

MOM: That's not so long.

AMY: I just can't get them.

MOM: Can you think of another way to solve it—a different strategy from what you've been doing?

AMY: I've tried everything I can think of.

MOM: Why don't you look through the examples in your math book? Maybe there will be some similar problems and you'll get some ideas from looking at how they were solved.

Amy's mom suggested a strategy, clearly implying that she believed Amy could figure out how to solve the problems if she spent a little more time and tried a different method. Brandon's dad, on the other hand, reinforced Brandon's view that solving hard math problems requires native intelligence.

PROMOTING GET-SMART RATHER THAN BORN-SMART BELIEFS

Here are additional ways to promote in your child the idea that effort and persistence lead to competence:

Send "Get-Smart" Messages

Emphasize notions of flexible intelligence. Tell your child, in every way you can, that brainpower is something you acquire. Make the following sayings (or their age-appropriate equivalents) your family mantras:

- Success is 1 percent inspiration, 99 percent perspiration.
- Geniuses are made, not born.

Avoid referring to IQ, "giftedness," "stupidity," or any other notion of fixed intelligence, such as

- "Your aunt isn't very bright, but she's sweet."
- "Johnny Moyer is a real brain. That whole family is really brainy."
- "Your friend is nice. Is she smart? Which reading group is she in?"
- "You must have inherited your intelligence from your Uncle Harry; it sure didn't come from your dad or me."

Emphasize effort as the route to competence:

- "If you keep doing those math puzzles, pretty soon you'll know more math than the teacher!"
- "You've really been working hard on spelling. Before you know it you'll be a real whiz."

Encourage and Praise Persistence

- "I'm so impressed with your determination. You're not going to give up until you figure this out, are you?"
- "I know you can do it if you keep at it."
- "If you approach your science with the same persistence that you've shown in social studies, you'll learn a lot and do very well."

If your child doesn't try very hard in school, praise *any* evidence of effort, even when it doesn't produce success. Give your daughter a word of praise simply for beginning her homework. If she has difficulty finishing, encourage her with a chocolate chip cookie and a friendly comment: "You're working so hard, I thought you deserved a treat." Your message is clear: trying counts.

Don't let poor results distract you from praising effort. If your son doesn't even get honorable mention in the science fair, tell him how proud you are of the effort he put into his project, and point out what he learned.

Point Out "Get-Smart" Role Models

Share information on your child's favorite musician or writer. Find out, for example, how many years he played an instrument before cutting his first CD, or how many books she wrote before she published one.

Tell your child stories about people who achieved great success through heroic efforts. When you watch TV or see a movie or a play together, point out the role of persistence and effort in a character's success.

When your child is little, read him *The Little Engine That Could* and Aesop's fable about the turtle and the hare. When he's older, read him stories about Marie Curie, Abraham Lincoln, and others who have achieved a goal through persistence.

Highlight the role of effort and persistence in your own achievements:

- "I type fast because I've been practicing typing since I was twelve years old."
- "I got that raise because of all the evening courses I took."
- "It took me all weekend to finish my taxes, but it was worth it. I feel like I've really accomplished something."
- "It wasn't luck that got me that promotion. I've been working toward it for five years!"

Why It May Be Difficult to Convince Our Children They Can "Get Smarter"

When UCLA psychologist Jim Stigler wanted to compare the persistence of American and Japanese elementary school students, he gave the same insoluble math problems to small groups of Japanese and American kids the same age. Most of the American kids struggled briefly with the problem and then gave up. The Japanese kids, in contrast, kept trying. And trying. And trying. In fact, they kept trying so long, remembers Stigler, that he felt very uneasy. "This is inhumane," he thought. "I have to stop them. They'll go on forever." So he halted the experiment, which had illustrated a cultural difference a little too sharply. "The Japanese kids assumed that if they kept working, they'd eventually get it," says Stigler. "The Americans thought, 'Either you get it or you don't.'"[6]

If you feel like you're swimming upstream when you're trying to persuade your child that effort and persistence are more important than native ability, it may help to remember that we, as a culture, tend to emphasize, if not worship, inborn talent.

To be sure, Americans honor hard work, as illustrated by our Horatio Alger stories and children's books like *The Little Engine That Could* (although luck was also crucial to the success of every young Alger hero).[7] Many American parents imply that effort is key when they tell their children, "You can be whatever you want to be." But too often a tendency to worship inborn talent eclipses our belief in hard work.

Jim Stigler plumbed the cultural differences when he asked fifth-graders in three countries whether they agreed with the statement, "The tests you take can show how much or how little natural ability you have." The kids in Taiwan disagreed with the statement, and the Japanese students disagreed strenuously, but the Americans agreed.[8]

Reverence for hard work has deep roots in Japanese and Chinese cultures. Confucian philosophy stresses self-improvement, and Chinese children are often told the poet Li Po's tale of the woman who was so persistent she ground a piece of iron into a needle. Another well-known fable tells about an old man and his sons who removed two mountains with a hoe (although God also intervened and helped out).

When an American can't do math, Stigler says, he's likely to say, "I don't have a head for numbers," but an Asian or Japanese person will say, "I haven't worked hard enough at math." Japanese and Chinese

When it comes to academics, Americans typically think that inborn ability is more important than effort and persistence. We also often think that ability and effort are inversely related—that the more effort you have to exert to succeed, the less intelligent you must be. This notion gives effort a bad name. "Our image of the truly gifted person," says UCLA psychologist Sandra Graham, "is one who doesn't have to work very hard."[9]

Thus when he was a Harvard freshman, says Bill Gates, "My whole thing was to sign up for classes and then not show up, because I didn't want to look like I was trying too hard."[10] In other words, Gates wanted to appear so smart that he didn't have to actually put in the effort of attending classes.

Another scholar thinks America's culture emphasizes luck (which we can't control) over hard work: "Even Horatio Alger realized that luck is as important as pluck," says Rutgers University historian Jackson Lears. "Look back at these classic tales of American success, and you will find that the key event in every young hero's rise to respectability is a fortuitous event that is beyond his control, the intervention of a wealthy benefactor at a crucial moment or saving an innocent heiress from Bowery toughs."[11]

elementary school teachers, he adds, tell their students that anyone who thinks long enough about a problem will find its solution. That's one reason, Stigler believes, that he and his colleagues found that Japanese and Chinese elementary school students outperform American students in both math and reading.

So keep in mind that it may be difficult at first (after all, you are bucking deeply rooted culture) when you try to instill "get-smart" beliefs in your child. But keep at it—with a little effort and persistence, you'll succeed.

When the pitcher Hideki Irabu was in his first season as a Yankee, a reporter asked his stepfather what Irabu was like as a boy. Hideki always wanted to be a pitcher, his stepfather replied. As a youngster he had even tied a rubber tube to a pole and pulled on it with a pitching motion to strengthen his arm and back muscles.

"He would wake up at 5:30 in the morning, earlier than we got up, to go out for a running exercise," Ichiro Irabu said. "He would tenaciously hang onto things that normal kids would have long given up. I was just stunned by his ability to keep up with a lot of hard work. And that made me think that he might grow up to be an extraordinary man."[12]

Wouldn't an American whose child had just been drafted by the Yankees credit his son's athletic talent?

Pay Special Attention When Your Child Is a Girl

Susan B. Anthony was fuming. At a recent meeting a man had proclaimed, "Woman's inherent nature is Love and man's Wisdom," she wrote to her fellow suffragist Elizabeth Cady Stanton in 1859.

"The discussion has been loud and long and how I wished that you could be there," she told her friend. "I tell you, Mrs. Stanton, after all, it is very precious to the soul of man, that he shall *reign supreme in intellect,* and it will take centuries if not ages to dispossess him of the fancy that he is born to do so."[13]

Perhaps the remnants today of such beliefs in women's inferior intelligence—which rest on the assumption that intelligence is fixed—helps explain why girls, especially bright girls, are more likely than boys to act "helpless" and quit in the face of difficult schoolwork. (For example, in Dweck's "red herring" study described at the beginning of this chapter, the higher the girls' IQs, the worse they did after the gobbledygook paragraph.)[14]

Why are girls less likely to persist when they face academic obstacles? Dweck has found that about equal numbers of girls and boys believe you have to be "born smart." But, as we saw in chapter 4, many more girls than boys have low confidence in their ability. When high-confidence kids think you have to be born smart, they do okay, since their confidence assures them they were born with enough brain-power to meet academic challenges. But girls who believe that you have to be born smart *and* that they missed the boat when brains were handed out are the most likely to become helpless when faced with a challenge.

This phenomenon among girls may not show up until middle school, when work usually becomes more challenging. But you can protect your daughter from this crippling combination of ideas by promoting her self-confidence, as I recommended in chapter 4, and by making sure early on that she believes she can "get smart" if she works hard.

Minorities May Also Be Especially Harmed by "Born-Smart" Beliefs

In 1916 Stanford University professor of education Lewis Terman wrote that "no amount of school instruction" could ever make many laborers and servant girls

> intelligent voters or capable voters in the true sense of the word. . . . The fact that one meets this type with such frequency among Indians, Mexicans, and negroes [sic] suggests quite forcibly that the whole question of racial differences in mental traits will have to be taken up anew and by experimental methods. The writer predicts that when

this is done there will be discovered enormously significant racial differences in general intelligence.[15]

Ten years later a Columbia Teachers College professor, Leta Hollingworth, added that "American children of Italian parentage show a low average of intelligence. The selection of Italians received into this country has yielded very few gifted children."[16]

As this snippet of history shows, minorities and immigrants have long faced social messages of intellectual inferiority similar to those encountered by women—messages that rest on an implicit belief that intelligence is fixed and inborn. As with girls, when minority students are hit with the double whammy of a "born-smart" belief that intersects with the insidious myth of racial intellectual inferiority, they are likely to falter.

Stanford psychology professor Claude Steele recently showed how this stigma operates even in high-achieving minority students. He and his colleague Joshua Aronson gave the advanced Graduate Record Examination (GRE) in literature to a group of black and white Stanford sophomores with the same intellectual ability (as measured by their SAT scores). They told the students that the purpose of the test was to determine their verbal ability. Steele and his colleague chose the GRE because they thought it would be particularly hard for these students, who were mostly sophomores, and that the black students might be intimidated by the stereotype—that is, that they would interpret the difficulty as evidence of their inferior intellectual ability. Indeed, black students performed "dramatically less well than white students" on the exam, says Steele. However, when the same test was given to another group of equally matched students who were told that its purpose was to study their problem-solving methods, the black students' scores equaled those of the white students. "When you remove stereotype threat from the testing situation, by representing the test as 'nondiagnostic' of ability, black students' performance goes up dramatically," says Steele. Subsequent studies showed that this "stereotype threat" can depress the test scores of other groups too: women who take math tests, for example, or white males who believe they are being measured against Asian students.[17]

Of course, there is no sound evidence for differences in intelligence based on race. Although there are different averages on IQ tests if one examines them by race (and definitions of race are by no means clear), study after study has shown that IQ test scores strongly reflect the test taker's experiences, and that differences in experience explain such variations.[18] Given that racial bias still exists in many people's minds, however, if your child is a minority, it's especially important to instill in him both self-confidence and the belief that he can get smart by working hard.

Researchers at Washington University in St. Louis compared the IQs of American black and white college students during their senior year in high school and at college graduation. Using the large database of the National Longitudinal Survey of Youth, they found that IQs of black students who went to college increased four times as much as those of white students. Researchers hypothesized that inferior schooling caused a gap (as much as 15 points) in high school but that college leveled the playing field.[19]

It's Worth the Effort

Realizing that hard work and persistence make her "smarter" will rev up your child's inner motivation to learn, since she'll see that putting out effort makes sense. But that's not the only effect of your child's beliefs about intelligence. In the next chapter we'll see some other positive effects of "get-smart" beliefs on your child's school achievement and desire to learn.

The notion of inborn intelligence or IQ is an American invention and is deeply embedded in our culture. In the early 1900s, Alfred Binet was asked by the French ministry of public instruction to develop a reliable method for identifying children who should be enrolled in special schools in Paris. In 1905 Binet, then director of the Psychological Laboratory at the Sorbonne, and his colleague Théodore Simon invented an exam to accomplish that task. Binet was horrified when Americans started using his test to measure inborn intelligence. "A few modern philosophers," Binet wrote in 1909, "seem to lend their moral support to [certain] deplorable verdicts when they assert that an individual's intelligence is a fixed quantity, a quantity which cannot be increased. We must protest and react against this brutal pessimism."

Binet's own experience made him particularly sensitive to the notion of inflexible intelligence. When he took his baccalaureate exam, the extensive all-or-nothing test French teenagers must pass to enter a university, he had confused the name of a Greek philosopher with one of the characters in a classic fable by La Bruyère. His examiner for the oral test, Mme. Martha, lashed out at him furiously. "She declared that I would never have a philosophical mind," he wrote later. " 'Never.' What a strong word!"[20]

8

Getting Smart or Looking Smart?
Your Child's Goals Make All the Difference

Six-year-old Tiffany gets into the car, buckles her seat belt, and takes a box of raisins from her lunch box.

> MOM: Well, how was your third day of second grade?
> TIFFANY (*popping raisins into her mouth*): We got reading groups. I'm in the Tigers.
> MOM (*dying to know the group level*): Which group is that?
> TIFFANY: We read the green books.
> MOM (*knitting brow*): Who else is in your group?
> TIFFANY: Shawna, Clark, Samantha, Jessie, and David.
> MOM: Oh, good. That must be the high reading group.

You can hardly blame Tiffany's mom for wanting to know how her daughter stacks up against other kids. It's understandable—especially since performance pressures are greater now than they have ever been. Admission to preschool and college alike has become highly competitive, and no family is immune from the pressure. Some affluent parents in big cities start test prepping when their children are toddlers, so they can win a slot in the most prestigious preschools. Family life deteriorates from the cramming that children later do to get into the best high schools, while worried kids react with anxiety symptoms ranging from nail biting to drugs, from passively "checking out" to full-fledged rebellion.

Of course you want your child to do well in school. And it is perfectly reasonable to want your child to "look smart" by scoring high on tests and by getting good grades. But how does the goal of performing affect your child's love of learning? Does it fire up his inner desire to learn or throw cold water on it?

Performance Goals and Learning Goals

The emphasis on "looking smart" or performing well in school is closely linked to the belief that intelligence is inborn and unchangeable. Because our culture places a high value on intelligence, kids who believe you are born smart or not tend to put a premium on appearing smart (or at least avoiding looking dumb). In other words, they tend to stress "performance goals," which means that doing well and looking intelligent are more important to them than actually learning material. If your child cares more about getting a good grade on a math test than about understanding the math concepts being tested, she has a performance goal.

Kids who believe you can "get smart," on the other hand, usually emphasize "learning goals." They tend to focus on gaining knowledge and skills, on *getting smart* rather than on *looking smart*. So if your child focuses on understanding math concepts, she has a learning goal.

Everybody has both learning and performance goals. You may remember, for example, simultaneously wanting to learn how to write well and wishing for a good grade on your compositions. Similarly, maybe you now belong to a book club, and while you enjoy learning from the reading, you also hope the group finds your comments intelligent. Perhaps when you were in school you had different goals for different subjects: you wanted to learn about history, but in science you cared only about earning a passing grade.

In the same way, most children have *both* learning goals and performance goals. They may study to learn, but they also want a certain grade—perhaps to make the honor roll or perhaps simply to avoid embarrassment.

There's nothing inherently wrong with performance goals. In fact, they're desirable and necessary. Kids often have to "show" they've learned one thing to go on to the next and, as Carol Dweck says, "all students want to be validated for their skills and their accomplishments."[1] The problem arises when kids *overemphasize* performance goals. Ironically, when students focus more on how they're performing than on what they're learning, they perform less well.

Kids Do Better with Learning Goals

Studies have demonstrated repeatedly that kids with learning goals both learn better and enjoy it more. Purdue University psychologist Dale Schunk, for example, gave math problems to a group of fourth-graders. He told half of the kids, "You'll be trying to *learn* how to solve fraction problems when the denominators are the same." The others were told, "You'll be trying to *solve* fraction problems when the denominators are the same." Surprisingly, this slight difference in directions affected children's approach to the problems markedly. The kids who were instructed to learn not only expressed more self-confidence before starting, but they also solved significantly more problems—an average of fourteen, compared to eleven problems for the children who were told simply to "solve" the problems (that is, to perform well).[2]

DEEPER THINKING

Other studies have shown that learning goals promote deeper under-standing than performance goals. In one study, UCLA researchers San-dra Graham and Shari Golan asked a group of fifth- and sixth-graders to answer questions that appeared on their computer screens for six seconds. Some of the questions called for superficial rhyming answers; others required more complex thinking. The researchers told one-third of the children simply to answer the questions by filling in the blank, and another third that the exercise would show "how good" they were at problem solving. The final third were told only to have fun and enjoy the challenge.[3]

All three groups scored the same on the easy rhyming questions. But children who received the instructions that focused on "how good they were" scored lower than the other two groups on the questions that required deeper thinking.

BETTER MOTIVATION

Finally, study after study has shown that children enjoy academic work more and their internal motivation flourishes when their primary focus is learning. In one study, for example, Carol Ames and Jennifer Archer asked 176 kids in grades eight through eleven to fill out one question-naire about the climate of their classroom and another about how much they liked the class. Some kids reported that the climate mainly promoted learning. They agreed with statements like "The teacher wants us to try new things," "The teacher wants us to learn how to solve problems on our own," and "Students don't care about the grades other students get." Others indicated that the atmosphere stressed per-forming, agreeing with statements like "Students compete against each other to get high grades," "Students try hard to get the highest grade," or "Students know if they're doing better or worse than the other students." The more the children felt the classroom climate focused on learning, the more they liked the class.[4]

Why Learning Goals Work Better

Researchers have found that learning goals are superior to performance goals for several reasons.

BETTER LEARNING TECHNIQUES

One reason is that kids who focus on learning rather than on performing tend to study "actively." For example, they review material they don't understand, ask questions as they work, and connect present and past learning. Students who emphasize performance, on the other hand, tend to use "passive" and superficial strategies, such as copying, guessing, and skipping hard questions.[5] They also take shortcuts or do only what is necessary to get a good grade. If no other strategy for looking smart is available, they may even cheat.

LESS ANXIETY

Performance goals can create tremendous anxiety. Do you remember watching another student turn in his test and walk out of the classroom while you were struggling through it? Perhaps you barely noticed, but when four other classmates followed him, you may have started panicking and had trouble concentrating. Perhaps you ended up spending more time watching others finish than working on your own test.

Kids concerned with looking smart suffer from this kind of anxiety all the time. Instead of listening to what the teacher is saying, they worry he will call on them and they won't know the answer. Their minds fill with anxious self-preoccupation. As one little girl said when asked how she felt while doing math problems, "I was nervous, I thought maybe I wouldn't know how to do things. I was mostly thinking I was making a fool of myself."[6]

In short, researchers have found that the more time children spend worrying about how smart they look, the less attention they are able to give to actually getting smart.

BROADER SCOPE OF ATTENTION

"Will that be on the test, Miss Crabtree?" This age-old question illustrates how studying only to get a good grade narrows students' learning to what they expect to be tested on.

You may have heard comments from your child like the following: "I don't have to learn that, Mom. It won't be on the test," or "I don't have to check the spelling. Mrs. Mahoney doesn't take off for spelling." Obviously, such attitudes cut learning off at the pass.

Soon after I moved to Los Angeles, I decided to take an adult night school Spanish class. The atmosphere was noncompetitive, but I wasn't able to shed old performance concerns. The teacher routinely gave us a set of questions printed on a page and asked each student a question, going in the order in which we sat around a table. I would count down to find out my question, and rehearse my answer over and over while he moved around the table. When my turn came, I was able to look competent because I was so well rehearsed. But I missed learning from the other students' questions and answers. Perhaps this is why I still can't speak Spanish.

WILLINGNESS TO ASK FOR HELP

Children concerned about looking smart think that seeking help is tantamount to announcing, "I don't get it," or even worse, "I'm stupid." Indeed, research has shown that kids with performance goals shrink from asking for help when they need it. Three University of Michigan psychologists, for example, rated the climate of several fifth-grade classrooms as "learning oriented" or "performance oriented." Then they gave a questionnaire to students that asked them to rate how "true" for them were statements like "If my math work is too hard for me, I just don't do it rather than ask for help." Sure enough, the kids in classrooms where performing was emphasized over learning showed the most reluctance to ask for help.[7]

APPROPRIATE STANDARDS

Does your child ever check her homework three times, rewrite a paper over and over, or study obsessively for a quiz? Sometimes kids who are overly concerned with their performance learn the same thing over and over rather than moving on to more challenging material. Anxious about their inner ability, petrified of making mistakes, and determined to get an A every time, the perfectionist student never feels like she's studied enough.

Perfectionism, the ultimate in performance goals, may ensure good grades, but it limits learning. That's because the time a perfectionist spends going over already-learned concepts is time away from learning more challenging material.

RELISHING CHALLENGES

When I was a high school senior, I was invited to take calculus along with fourteen other high-achieving students. The first day of class we took a test to tell the teacher how much we knew. My score was the lowest in the class, and my fragile confidence wilted.

That afternoon I dropped calculus. It didn't occur to me to stick it out because I would learn something and maybe even enjoy the challenge. All I could think was that I'd ruin my GPA.

Years later I realized I'd had an extreme case of *performance goalitis*. It wasn't that I couldn't do the work, since I took calculus the next year as a college freshman (when it was required) and did fine. It was simply that in high school I was so preoccupied with getting good grades I shied away from challenges.

Perhaps the worst problem with performance goals, as my experience and many studies illustrate, is that they can make children avoid challenging work. As I've stressed throughout this book, not only are "just-right" challenges key to stretching a student's learning, but they are also crucial for keeping alive your child's self-motivation. Emphasizing learning goals will encourage your child to tackle difficult work and make qualitative leaps in learning. When she does a good job on a challenging assignment, the enjoyment and pride she feels will keep her internal desire to learn burning steady and bright.

Carol Dweck will never forget a boy in one of her studies who, when he got to a difficult problem, acted like he'd been given a chocolate bar. "He pulled up his chair," she says, "rubbed his hands together, smacked his lips, and said 'I love a challenge.'"[8] The boy was a "get-smart" student who, instead of worrying about how intelligent he looked, found it exciting to take risks.

Working Overtime to Avoid Looking Dumb

Have you ever played Scrabble or chess while projecting the image that you're not trying? Perhaps you remarked, "I'm having trouble concentrating," or thumbed through a magazine during your opponent's turn.

Or did you ever announce, just before a teacher handed out a test, that you didn't feel well or hadn't had a chance to study? These are the same tactics children use to avoid looking dumb. The reasoning behind them is simple: if you do well and you're not really concentrating or you haven't studied, you must be a real brain. If you *don't* perform well— well, even smart people don't succeed when they're distracted or sick.

Kids with performance goals who fear they can't succeed in school frequently use these kinds of ruses to make sure that, if they fail, they can blame it on something other than lack of smarts. Some children spend more energy managing the impression they're making on others than they do on learning.

Perhaps your child uses none of the methods below. But if he does, it means he's working overtime to avoid looking incompetent. If you've seen one or more of the following, it's a signal for you to shore up your child's belief that getting smart is more important than looking smart. Here are some of the most common "impression management" techniques (also called "self-handicapping" strategies) to watch out for:

- *Procrastination.* If he fails, he can blame it on his belated studying.
- *Lost and eaten homework.* If she doesn't think she can do her homework, she can save face by "forgetting" it, or claiming the dog ate it. (Takes the focus off her ability and puts it on "lack of organization" or "unruly animal.")
- *Unattainable goals.* He's sure to fail, but since the goals were so high, failing doesn't reflect on his ability.
- *Very low goals.* Your child may tell you he expects to fail his spelling test, hoping you will then be happy with a C.
- *Excuses.* She may provide explanations for low performance other than low ability: "I had a stomachache." "John was bothering me."
- *Halfhearted effort.* If he doesn't try, failing doesn't mean he's stupid. No one knows how well he might have done had he actually put some effort into it. He'll get criticized for not trying, but that's better than having people think he is incompetent.

Helping Your Child Emphasize Learning Goals and Getting Smart

You can help your child focus on learning rather than performing. First, however, you have to make sure that *you* think people can get smart, and that learning is more important than looking good—because it's impossible to persuade a child of something you don't believe yourself.

Here's a quiz to help you test your own beliefs:[9]

1. Would you prefer your child to
   a. Do well in school even though he doesn't work very hard? *or*
   b. Work hard in school even though he doesn't do very well?

2. Which for you is the more important sign of doing well in school?
   a. Getting good grades, *or*
   b. Showing improvement in skills and knowledge?

3. If your child is doing well, which is the best explanation?
   a. My child is bright.
   b. My child works hard.
   c. My child's teacher is very good.
   d. The work is easy.

4. If your child isn't doing very well in school, which is the best explanation?
   a. My child is not very bright.
   b. My child doesn't work hard enough.
   c. My child's teacher could be better.
   d. The work is very hard.

If you answered (b) three or more times, you believe that effort counts more than native ability in school. If you answered (b) only one or twice, you need an Intelligence Beliefs Makeover. You can give yourself one by reading over chapter 7 again and discussing it with a spouse or friend. You can also resolve to work hard to implement my advice in the sections below, which show you how to ensure that your child has "get-smart" beliefs and emphasizes learning goals.

Which Kids Suffer Most from Performance Goals?

Overstressing performance goals can harm anyone, but there are two types of kids who suffer most: bright students and kids with low confidence. Bright kids who are mostly concerned with getting good grades, praise, and other honors and who don't have to work very hard for them can end up bored and unmotivated. Why should they challenge themselves if they can reach their goals without much effort?

Kids who have performance goals *and* doubt their ability to succeed in school suffer from an academic knockout punch: why should they exert effort since they will look stupid no matter what they do?

Promoting Learning Goals in Your Child

Let's look at the way parents promote either learning or performance goals by listening to two parents dealing with their daughters' math exams:

DAD #1: How did you do on your math test?
COURTNEY: Okay.
DAD #1: What grade did you get?
COURTNEY: Well, I got three wrong.
DAD #1: Is that an A or a B?
COURTNEY: I don't know. I just know I got three wrong.
DAD #1: Well, how did your friends do? What did Mikey get?
COURTNEY: I think he got four wrong.

DAD #2: Hi honey! How are you doing?

MICHELLE: Okay.

DAD #2: How was school?

MICHELLE: We got our math tests back.

DAD #2: Oh, you did?

MICHELLE: I got three wrong.

DAD #2: How many did you get right?

MICHELLE: All the rest. Like ten maybe.

DAD #2: Well, that's pretty good. Did you understand why you got the three wrong?

MICHELLE: Not really.

DAD #2: Do you want to look at them together? Maybe we can figure out what you don't understand.

I'm sure you guessed that Michelle's dad was the one encouraging learning goals. Of course, like Courtney's dad, you also want to know how your child is performing. After all, grades do make a difference. But do your best to avoid "how did you do?" as your first question.

SHOWING YOUR CHILD YOU VALUE "GETTING SMART"

Here are some other ways to encourage your child to emphasize learning:

Stress the Importance of Learning as a Goal

- "I'd rather you work really hard, learn something, and get a B, than breeze easily through things you already know and get an A."
- "Which assignment should you choose? Well, which one will teach you more?"
- "If you join the scouts you'll probably learn some really interesting things."

- "We signed you up for the magnet school because you'll learn a lot of math and science there."

Highlight Learning More Than Grades

- Ask your child, "What did you learn today in school?" five times for every "How did you do?"
- Ask questions about the material your child is studying. "What is your social studies unit about?"
- Focus on understanding. Ask your child, "Will you show me how you figured out this math problem?" rather than "Did you get this one right?"
- When your daughter brings home a paper with mistakes or missing answers, encourage her to learn by correcting the errors and completing unfinished problems.

Point Out Experiences That Helped You or Your Child to Learn

- "When I worked on Grandpa and Grandma's farm, I learned how to milk cows. And watching the animals give birth was a terrific biology lesson."
- "What I loved about our trip was learning about the trees and plants when we took the hike with the forest ranger."

PROFITING FROM MISTAKES

Once I watched videotapes of two math lessons. In the first, an American math teacher wrote a problem on the board and called on kids for the answer. If an answer was wrong, the teacher ignored it and called on other students until one of them gave the correct answer.

The second tape showed a class of Japanese fifth-graders learning how to add fractions with unequal denominators. The teacher asked the students to add one-third to one-half. She called on a boy, who answered, "Two-fifths." Instead of ignoring his mistake and calling on another child, the teacher lingered over this mistake, guiding her students to understand the root of the problem. "Which is larger," she asked them, "two-fifths or one-half?" "Isn't it strange," she continued, "that you could add a number to one-half and get a number that is smaller than one-half?"[10] Rather than acting as though mistakes are shameful, the teacher used the child's error to develop the students' understanding.

We can learn from this Japanese teacher's attitude toward mistakes. One of the most important differences between "look-smart" kids and "get-smart" kids is the way they think about errors. If your child concentrates on looking smart, she'll be chagrined by mistakes, which call her intelligence into question. But if she's working to learn, she'll know that she can benefit from her mistakes because they tell her what she doesn't understand yet, or what she needs to learn next.

Here's how to help your child appreciate the value of his mistakes.

Explain That Mistakes Are a Natural Part of Learning

- "Nobody ever learns anything new without making mistakes."
- "Remember, it took scientists seventy-seven tries before they cloned a sheep."

Model a Positive Attitude toward Your Own Blunders

- Instead of berating yourself, treat your mistake as a lesson. "Oh, no! I forgot to pay the credit card bill again. I'm going to write a reminder on the calendar from now on."
- Tell stories about mistakes you made: "I remember getting a 50 in a spelling test in third grade. But I studied really hard and the next week I brought my grade up to 85. Boy, did I feel terrific."

- When you try something very difficult and fail, praise yourself for try-ing. "I didn't get that job, but applying was a good learning experi-ence. I'm proud of myself for trying, and now I know what I have to do next time."
- Tell your child about your all-time favorites—mistakes that taught you the best lessons. "One of my worst mistakes in fifth grade was not telling anyone I didn't know how to do long division. I got more and more confused in math, and almost failed it that semester. Ever since I realized that I was silly, and I've made a point of saying what I don't understand and getting help."

Help Your Child Learn from His Mistakes and Failures

- "Let's go over all the questions you got wrong on your social studies test and see if we can figure out exactly what you're confused about."
- "I wonder if we can find out what went wrong in your science project. Any ideas why the seeds you planted didn't grow?"
- "I've circled all the grammar mistakes. See how many you can fix, and then we'll go over the others together so we know exactly what you still have to learn."

Don't Tolerate Siblings or Anyone Else Making Fun of Each Other's Mistakes

- "We don't think mistakes are stupid in this family."
- "Your job is to help your brother, not tease him."

COMBINING LEARNING AND PERFORMANCE GOALS SMOOTHLY

I hope this chapter has convinced you that an indirect strategy of help-ing your child focus on learning as her goal is the best way to improve her grades and raise her test scores, as well as to protect her from the anxiety of pressure to perform. I understand that the "real world" is

IN PRAISE OF FAILURE

- Director Alan Pakula's wife, Hannah, says that when she began writing biographies he encouraged her to experiment. "Alan said, 'It's OK. Fall flat on your face.' That was an enormous gift. He gave me his protection. He honored work, successful or not."[11]
- Engineers seek out failure, says Duke University professor of civil engineering Henry Petroski. "We rely on failure of all kinds being designed into many of the products we use every day," he writes. Failure is often a "desirable end."[12]
- Some American businesses like to hire people who have faltered, because it shows they can take risks and have learned some important lessons. Failure has particularly strong cachet in Silicon Valley. "Failure is as much a credential as success—even, perhaps, more so," says David Cowan, a Menlo Park, California, venture capitalist. "If [they] are coming off a failed business, they have an innate understanding of the consequences of running out of cash, and they focus on long-term issues earlier on than other people."[13]

increasingly full of such pressures, which are not always easy to balance with a love of learning. When your child is worried about a high-stakes test, or if your community is one of those in which parents are talking about "name brand" colleges while children are still in elementary school, try not to panic. Do what is necessary to meet the long-term goal—sign up for the high-stakes test or the necessary course of study. But after that, keep your focus and your child's as much as possible on the next learning goal in view: reading that book, writing that report, learning that piano piece, or mastering that long division. Concentrate on mastering knowledge and skills step-by-step: it's the best way to keep calm and, in the long run, to achieve high scores as well as to acquire a love of learning.

Competition: Does It Increase
Your Child's Desire to Learn?

Anna and Danielle had been best friends since kindergarten. They sat together at lunchtime, jumped rope together at recess, and played at each other's homes on weekends. Their mothers became friends too, and frequently compared the girls' progress in school.

As they approached fourth grade, Anna started shooting ahead of Danielle academically. Danielle's mother held Anna up as a model, urging Danielle to get good grades "like Anna." Sometimes she even set up a competition. "Put everything you've got into your report on Arizona," she told her daughter. "Maybe you can beat out Anna for a change."

One day the girls' fourth-grade teacher saw Anna sitting on a bench in the schoolyard, crying. "What happened?" asked the teacher. "Danielle's not my friend anymore, because you put me in the high math group and she's in the middle one," sobbed Anna. Wiping the little girl's tears away, her teacher told her that being in different groups wasn't a reason not to be friends. Suspecting there was more to this story, the teacher called both girls' parents to a conference. She asked them not to compare their daughters' progress, because the resulting competition was interfering with the girls' friendship. And she counseled the parents to praise Anna's and Danielle's efforts whenever they tried hard, regardless of the other girl's achievements. The parents followed her advice and soon the girls were fast friends again.

FOCUSES ATTENTION ON PERFORMANCE

Most of us think that competition is healthy and motivates children to learn. In that spirit, many schools sponsor contests for prizes, awards, scholarships, and trophies. Unfortunately, however, this kind of competition often smothers children's love of learning rather than nurturing it. That's because competition focuses children's attention on performance—on winning rather than on learning.

DISCOURAGES EFFORT

Competition in school has another important downside. Since students start with vastly different skills and abilities, it's rarely fair. That's why (as you may remember from your own school experience) academic contests usually motivate only a handful of outstanding students. Kids who believe they can't win have no reason to try.

Like other forms of academic competition, grading on a curve and recognizing only the "best" papers by putting them on the bulletin board motivate only a few students. I'm not saying excellent papers should never be praised or used as models for other children to aspire to. But when the praise is public and only a few children can realistically hope to be recognized, it can discourage rather than motivate effort.

If, on the other hand, a teacher defines as "outstanding" all work that has taken serious effort and represents excellent progress, then all children have a chance to be recognized. Everyone can't be "the best," but all students can work hard and increase their skills.

PROMOTES SUPERFICIAL WORK

Competition can promote hasty work—just what is needed to "win." I remember when my third-grade teacher put a "reading wheel" for each student on the bulletin board. They had slots to fill in with the titles of books we had read and summarized on book report forms she handed out. The public display of the wheels provoked my competitive instincts, and I was determined to beat the girl considered the best reader in the class. I wrote book reports fast and furiously. The problem was that I didn't really read the books. I just raced through them for the superficial information I needed to fill in the book report forms. I can't remember whether I won the race, but I do remember being more motivated to win than to read!

SQUELCHES CREATIVITY

Competition can also stifle creativity. Harvard University psychologist Teresa Amabile demonstrated this effect by throwing paper collage parties for two groups of girls, age seven to eleven. She told the first group that judges would award prizes to the three best designs, and the second group that three prizes would be raffled off at the end of their party. Then a panel of seven artists, working independently, rated the girls' designs. The collages of the girls who had not competed for prizes, they all agreed, were more varied, complex, and creative.

"Children who are competing with their peers," Amabile explained, may be "more conservative, less likely to take risks, less likely to explore and therefore less likely to do something that's creative."[14]

Making Competition Work

Competition is not all bad. You can help your child take advantage of the fun and excitement of fair competition, and minimize the harm from unfair competition. Here's how:

SET INDIVIDUAL GOALS

Encourage your child to set individual goals and compete with himself. "How many spelling words do you think you could get right this week?"

Help her draw a chart, tape it on the refrigerator, pin it on her bulletin board, or save it on the computer. She can mark her progress every day or week.

ENCOURAGE FRIENDLY COMPARISON

Encourage "friendly comparison," using a friend as a model rather than as someone to beat: "Alissa read *Little Women* and really liked it; I bet you could read it too."

FOCUS ON EFFORT AND LEARNING

When your child does well in a competition, praise her effort and creativity at least as much as the outcome. When your child fares poorly, don't say, "Next time you'll do better." Instead focus his attention on what he gained by participating: "You know more about electricity now than I do." "Look at how you got those flip turns down to get ready for this swim meet." "Think about all the new friends you made." And don't forget to praise him for taking on a challenge.

A fourth-grade teacher once told me how she cushions her students from discouragement while studying for the National Geography Bee, which only one student from each state can win. "I tell my students their goal is to 'be prepared,'" she told me. "I tell them studying for the bee teaches them a great deal, and that no matter who wins, it's an honor to participate."[15]

Cooperation Motivates More Than Competition

Kids enjoy working with other kids, and competition among groups is usually better than individual competition. University of Minnesota psychologist David Johnson examined hundreds of studies that compared cooperation and competition in school, and found that cooperative activities among students produced significantly higher academic achievement in 316 out of 351 cases. He also discovered 98 examples of pupils liking their lessons more while working cooperatively, but only 12 such examples when they were working competitively.[16]

Research has also shown that children think about their ability and "looking smart" when competing individually, but focus on effort when they compete with themselves or as part of a group.[17]

Many teachers today organize group work. Studies show that "cooperative learning," when structured properly, encourages kids to help each other learn. Talking to each other about the material forces them to organize their thinking and explain their ideas, which in turn helps them recognize and fill in the gaps in each other's understanding. All students benefit, regardless of skill level.

Some teachers combine cooperation with competition by creating groups of children to compete with each other. The teams are evenly matched on students' skill levels, so that all groups (and therefore all students) have a genuine chance of "winning." Team contests can foster feelings of cooperation and mutual appreciation, rather than the feelings of isolation sometimes evoked by individual competition. Competition that is fair, friendly, and low-key promotes great enthusiasm and energetic learning.

You can encourage your child to learn with his friends informally. Don't be too strict about your child hogging the phone, for example, if he is doing homework with a classmate.

If your child is having difficulty doing his homework, suggest he invite a friend over to work together. (You might check in occasionally to make sure they're not playing video games.) Doing schoolwork with a friend can be more fun, and the help they give each other can promote both children's learning. This kind of collaboration fine-tunes and consolidates the skills of the "helper" while giving the "helpee" the benefit of explanations from a peer, which sometimes are more understandable than an adult's.

If competition sometimes helps and sometimes hurts kids' self-motivation to learn, how about rewards and grades? In the next chapter I'll talk about their role in fostering children's love of learning.

9

Rewards and Grades:
Do They Help or Harm?

Once there was an old man who was exasperated by the noise of children playing near his house. It seemed like they were picking on him purposely, throwing their ball on his lawn, tossing pebbles against his door, and making a racket right under his living room window. One day he called a few of the boys over and offered to pay them a quarter to make as much noise as possible the next day. The kids were delighted. What could beat getting paid to do something you wanted to do anyway? True to his word, the following afternoon the man paid them each a quarter.

The next day the boys made noise again, but the man said he was short on change, and could pay them only twenty cents apiece. "Oh well," the kids thought. "That's better than nothing." But each day their pay dwindled a little more, until finally the old man said he was broke and wouldn't be able to pay them anymore. "What?!" the kids shouted back angrily. "You think we're gonna make noise for nothing?" And they refused to play near the old man's house ever again.[1]

Psychologists tell this story to illustrate how rewards can shift children's attention away from the intrinsic value of an activity to the reward itself as the reason for engaging in it. In other words, it demonstrates that the best way to undermine kids' interest in learning is to reward them for doing it.

Nevertheless, rewards for learning are everywhere. Some programs offer kids money to read books, others promise pizza. I've even heard of school principals who promise to dye their hair green, eat worms, dress as an alligator, or sit on the roof dressed as a clown if students will read a certain number of pages!

As a parent, you may be sympathetic to such ploys, because you've used rewards yourself. I certainly have. When Meredith was little, I promised her a cookie after dinner if she ate four bites of squash or drank all her milk. When she was in elementary school I once paid her to practice the multiplication tables.

Perhaps you've bribed your child with crayons to encourage potty training or a trip to a ball game for good grades. We've all used rewards at one time or another for a very simple reason: they work, at least in the short term.

Rewards aren't inherently bad. A bribe here and a prize there won't spoil for life your child's self-motivation to learn. But you do have to use them sparingly and wisely, or you may accomplish the opposite of what you intend.

Research has shown that rewards can be very effective for encouraging kids to do schoolwork. The psychologist H. Cohen, for example, set up a "token economy" for delinquent boys living in a group home. The boys received points for academic achievement, which they could exchange for clothes, magazines, or special privileges. Their academic achievement improved dramatically under this system.[2]

A. Alschuler did a similar study with a group of fifth-graders. Each student received $2,000 in play money and wrote and signed a contract, which included academic goals. If they missed a goal or turned an assignment in late, they had to return some money. The higher the goal, the greater the payoff. (This system encouraged the "just-right" challenges I explained in chapter 3.) In one year, these fifth-graders advanced an average of three years on standardized math test scores.[3]

Research on many "token economies" like these has shown that they're very effective—*as long as the adults in charge keep giving out the tokens.* But as the story of the Old Man and the Noisy Boys illustrates, using rewards to motivate children to learn has important pitfalls: first, your child's effort will stop when you stop dispensing the rewards. Second, when children have an internal desire to learn, offering a reward can extinguish it by shifting their attention away from the inherent enjoyment of learning and on to the reward itself.

Stanford psychologist Mark Lepper demonstrated this principle in his classic 1973 study. He and his colleagues gave Magic Markers to sixty preschoolers and divided the children into three groups. They told the first group that if they drew a picture they'd get a certificate with a gold star and a red ribbon on it. The second group wasn't told about the certificates, but received them after drawing their pictures. A third group neither knew about nor received rewards, but simply colored away happily.

Two weeks later the researchers returned, but this time they didn't offer any certificates. When these same children were given Magic Markers, those in the second two groups (which hadn't been told about a reward in the first session) spent as much time drawing as they had previously. (Notice that for the second group, giving an *unexpected* reward didn't squash their interest.) But the kids in the first group, who had received the awards as promised, spent only half as much time drawing as they had the first time around; their interest had plummeted. In addition, their pictures were sloppier and less creative than in the first session. These children were now "oriented not towards enjoying the activity for its own sake," explains Lepper, "but towards what they had to do to get the reward. So they quickly whipped up a picture."[4] More than fifty studies following Lepper's replicated his results.

Other studies show that focusing on a reward makes students narrow their focus of attention, forget what they've learned, fall back on "safe" strategies like memorization, and take shortcuts, including cheating. For example, psychologists Carole and Russell Ames tracked the results when a local restaurant promised a group of elementary school children coupons for a treat if they wrote four book reports in a month. The researchers found that to win the coupon the children chose short, easy, and even uninteresting books.[5]

University of California, Berkeley's Marty Covington puts it succinctly: "Learning becomes the way to obtain a reward," he says, "not a way to satisfy one's curiosity or to discover something of interest."[6]

Rewards can also discourage students from trying challenging work. University of Denver psychologist Susan Harter demonstrated this phenomenon when she gave a group of fifth- and sixth-graders anagram puzzles that were "very easy, easy, hard, and very hard" for them. She told half the kids that the puzzles were simply a game. However, the other half were told that they'd receive an A, B, C, or D grade.

A friend of mine gave story-writing software to her eight-year-old niece for her birthday. Katie spent days writing little stories, using the software to illustrate and print them, and gathering the stories into little books. She had quite a collection. Then one Saturday her aunt suggested Katie write personalized stories for neighbors and relatives, and sell them for a dollar. Her niece thought this was a terrific idea, and enthusiastically sold six stories in the first two weeks. But when sales petered out, she lost interest in writing stories and went back to playing with her Barbie dolls.

Children in the graded group chose significantly easier anagrams to work on.[7]

As Mark Lepper found in his Magic Marker study, rewards can stifle children's creativity. Harvard psychologist Teresa Amabile corroborated Lepper's finding when she asked a group of five- to ten-year-olds to make up a story as they turned the pages of a picture book without words. She told half the children that as a reward for telling the story they could take two instant camera pictures, if they first signed a contract promising to tell the story. The other children were simply allowed to take two instant pictures before they made up the tale. Later, three elementary school teachers listened to tape recordings of the stories and judged them. They rated the stories of the kids who hadn't signed the contract significantly more creative.[8] "People will be the most creative," says Amabile, "when they feel motivated primarily by the interest, enjoyment, satisfaction and challenge of the work itself—rather than by external pressures."[9]

Finally, rewards risk undercutting students' sense of control and responsibility over their schoolwork. Research has shown that bribes and incentives dampen children's feelings of autonomy, making them feel controlled by the person giving the rewards.[10]

When and How to Reward Your Child

Given the downside of rewards, you don't want to rely on them any more than you have to. But let's look first at the ways you *can* use rewards without undermining your child's motivation, achievement, or creativity.

USE REWARDS TO "JUMP-START" YOUR CHILD, IF ALL ELSE FAILS

I recently spoke to a group of elementary school parents, and a father volunteered this story:

My son loves to play basketball. Seth's a team player, which makes me happy, but last year he was taking his selfless play to the extreme, and wouldn't shoot! I explained to him that as a guard he was supposed to score, but he still wouldn't try it. Finally I offered him fifteen extra minutes of watching sports on TV for each basket he shot, up to two hours a week. At his next practice, Seth started shooting and made some baskets. That night he watched an hour and a half of TV sports. After that he just kept shooting, and we both forgot about the TV time.

As Seth's father found out, rewards are a good way to "jump-start" your child when he's reluctant to try something new. Similarly, a bribe can nudge your child to develop a skill until the feeling of competence itself brings her pleasure and motivation to continue. Once she develops some confidence and starts enjoying it, you can drop the reward.

Rewards can also motivate your child to master topics that may never be inherently interesting, like multiplication tables or spelling words. It's harmful to reward him for something he's already interested in. But if you've tried in vain to make a task more appealing, it's fine to bribe your child to learn something that doesn't interest him.

When you offer your child a reward as a "jump-start" or as a last resort, here are some tips to keep in mind:

- Give rewards that are meaningfully connected to the activity you're promoting. If you are trying to get your daughter to go to the museum,

At age eight Meredith became frustrated because her math homework was taking so long. I tried to make memorizing the multiplication tables fun by inventing a card game. It didn't work. Finally I paid her a penny for every set of numbers she wrote out.

offer to buy a coloring book about the Egyptians in the museum gift shop. If you're trying to get your son to finish his homework, promise to buy the automatic pencil he asked for if he finishes assignments every night for a week.

- Give the smallest reward that's effective. If an ice cream cone will work, don't offer a video game. The bigger the reward, the more it will shift your child's attention to the reward as the reason for doing the activity and the less likely he'll notice his own emerging interest.

- Don't create too great a delay between the promise of a reward and providing it. To a very young child, twenty minutes seems too far in the future; a ten-year-old might be able to wait a day.

When Meredith was in preschool I created a star chart to motivate her to get ready each morning. (I wasn't worried about spoiling her natural desire to get ready, because she didn't have any.) I promised a star for each time she got dressed on her own, and a toy after she earned ten stars. She lost interest after the first week, because it took too much time to earn the reward.

- Offer a reward or privilege you don't mind giving. Don't promise candy if you're concerned about her nutrition or extra television if you already think your daughter watches too much.

- Use language that recognizes your child has some choice or autonomy: "How about this: if you finish your homework for the next three nights, I'll bake you cookies. Would you agree to that?" "If you like, here's what we'll do: if you get at least a C on your next math test, I'll let you read comic books for fifteen minutes before you go to bed every night."

- Withdraw the reward as soon as your child shows an interest in the activity. You don't have to be explicit ("I guess I don't have to give you

> When Meredith heard that my parents had given my brothers and me a dollar for each A we earned in school, she asked if I'd do the same. Surprised that the price hadn't risen in forty years, I said yes; I didn't think the low value of the reward would detract from her intrinsic interest in schoolwork. I was right. The dollar was too small to shift her attention.

a dollar for every A anymore. You seem to be motivated to get them anyway.") Like Seth's dad, simply "forget."

Most important of all, don't use rewards if your child is already naturally motivated. The father of Zach's Little League teammate who offered players $5 for every home run meant well, but the kids were already trying as hard as they could to hit home runs. By offering them money, like the old man in the story, he risked squelching their internal motivation to hit homers.

Similarly, I haven't yet seen a five- or six-year-old who isn't excited about reading. So don't offer your first-grader a dollar for every book she reads. If she's not reading for pleasure, try other strategies. Make sure she has interesting books to read. Ask if she'd like to do her pleasure reading in the afternoon, right before bedtime, or on Saturday mornings, or if she'd like to sit with you and read every night.

USE REWARDS TO RECOGNIZE COMPETENCY

Far from squelching your child's love of learning, there's one particular kind of reward that's guaranteed to increase it: rewards conveying information about your child's competency. A certificate acknowledging she has mastered every piece in her piano book, a karate belt, or Girl Scout badge can make a child eager to go to the next level. That's because these rewards represent an accomplishment or a new skill. Rewards that give information about your child's new academic competencies will fire up his enthusiasm for school.

You can link a reward to your child's competency if you

- Accompany it with words: "I think you deserve a cookie for working so hard and making such a great map of Minnesota."
- Draw a certificate or make one on your computer: *This is to certify that Tricia Davila has mastered her addition facts.*

Downplay awards that reflect neither effort nor skill, like a pin given to every child in the school orchestra. (Or attach meaning to the pin by commenting on your child's specific achievement. "Your orchestra sounded great, and this pin will remind you of how much your flute playing improved this year.")

CONSIDER THE SUBTLE MESSAGE OF YOUR REWARD

I once visited a kindergarten teacher who demonstrated a way to use rewards very wisely. That morning she announced that if her students behaved very well, she would give them homework before they went home. The children were very excited by this possibility, and quieted down whenever she reminded them of her bribe. When the day was over, the students ran to their parents' happily waving the worksheets they'd "earned" by being especially good.

This savvy teacher was capitalizing on a sidelight of the Old Man and Noisy Boys Effect: when you offer a bribe, not only does your child's attention shift to it, but referring to something as a reward inflates its value. By making homework a reward, the teacher was cannily promoting the value of learning.

If, on the other hand, you offer your child a shopping trip for reading a book or an extra hour of sitcoms for watching a National Geographic show with you, your implied message is that neither the reading nor the educational TV show is pleasurable itself, but shopping and sitcoms have inherent value.

So if you're jump-starting your child with a reward, try offering him educational software, an extra bedtime story, a new book to read, or a chance to bake a cake with you.

Praise Works Better Than Rewards

Praise is intangible, but it can be just as effective as a movie or a pizza—especially when it conveys your warmth and approval and recognizes your child's competence.

Like rewards, praise nourishes your child's internal motivation to learn when it describes a new competency. So, as I mentioned in chapter 4, make sure that when you praise, your child knows exactly why you're praising her. When you praise your child,

- Be specific. "Good job" is nice, but "What nice neat handwriting!" or "Your story is really vivid. I can just see the forest" is even better.
- Praise only accomplishments that required effort. Praising your child for success at easy tasks will convey low expectations. Children know when they haven't tried hard, and may even feel embarrassed if you praise them for doing less than their best.
- Praise persistence. "I'm really proud of the way you stuck with this until you figured it out."
- Praise trying different strategies. "That new schedule you tried—doing a little homework before dinner—really seems to work for you. You've done a great job figuring out a strategy that works."
- Praise personal progress ("Your handwriting has improved," or "I

think you're starting to understand fractions now") rather than competitive standing ("I bet your handwriting is one of the best in the class"), or what she's done for you ("I'm really pleased at how well you're doing").

- Avoid praise that might make your child feel like she is being controlled or manipulated ("Good, you've done exactly what I wanted you to do"). Controlling language undermines feelings of autonomy (and therefore self-motivation).

- Praise behavior rather than the child. If your child finishes her homework and you praise her with "You're such a good girl!" you imply that your love and pride are conditional on her doing the work. In other words, she has to please you to maintain your love and acceptance. Instead of "You're a good girl!" or "I'm proud of you!" praise the behavior: "You must have tried really hard!" "You found a good way to do that."

- Avoid encouraging your child to become dependent on your praise. Help her evaluate her own work. For example, if your child comes to you with a picture he drew or a story he wrote, ask him, "What do you think of it?" "What do you like about it?" "Was it hard to draw (write)?" "Is that your best one so far, or do you like other pictures (stories) you've done better?"

- Don't overdo praise. Praising every two minutes will dilute its power. Don't praise everything your child says or does. If you say, "Nice job!" no matter what, you'll lose your credibility.

- Don't puff your child up with insincere praise just to make him "feel good." Really mean it. (Kids know the difference.)

Grades

As a child, Albert Einstein attended a militaristic German school where he did so poorly that the headmaster told his father it wouldn't matter what profession his son adopted. "He'll never make a success of any-thing," the headmaster scoffed. In his autobiography, Einstein com-plained about the school's emphasis on tests and grading:

> It is nothing short of a miracle that the modern methods of instruc-tion have not yet entirely strangled the holy curiosity of inquiry; for this delicate little plant, aside from stimulation, stands mainly in need of freedom; without this, it goes to wreck and ruin without fail. It is a very grave mistake to think that the enjoyment of seeing and searching can be promoted by means of coercion and sense of duty. . . . This coercion had such a deterring effect upon me that, after I had passed the final examination, I found the consideration of any scientific problem distasteful to me for an entire year.[11]

Later on, the future atomic physicist failed an entrance examination to a prestigious high school. He finally found a congenial academic atmosphere at a school he attended for remedial work. The teachers there structured learning around each student's search for knowl-edge.[12] In Einstein's case it took an entire year to recover, but his story shows how an excessive focus on tests and grades can damage your child's desire to learn.

Like rewards, grades shift a child's attention away from the content of what she is studying and on to the grade itself. Instead of concentrat-ing on the value and pleasure of learning about the workings of the human nervous system or how the Vikings built their boats, the graded student concentrates on the A she wants or the D she fears.

Many studies have demonstrated this effect. Psychologists Richard Ryan and Wendy Grolnick, for example, showed how grades can undermine students' interest in a topic when they asked fifth-graders in three schools to read a textbook selection about the history of farming. They told one-third of the kids, "We're going to test you on this mate-rial, and show your teacher your grade." Another third of the kids were told, "We're going to give you a test on this passage, but it's not for a grade." The final group was told simply to read the passage.

Later the students were tested on what they had learned and how they felt about it. Those in the two groups that hadn't been graded showed more interest in the history of farming, and had even grasped its concepts better than the kids in the group that had been graded. "The performance was better without the grade, and so was the interest and curiosity," explains Ryan. "Grades can be really undermining."[13]

The Japanese psychologist Masaharu Kage had similar results when he gave weekly math quizzes to a group of junior high school students. He told half the kids that the quizzes counted toward their final grade, and the other half that the quizzes were only to help them monitor their own learning. Not only did the second group show more interest in the material, but on the final exam they significantly outscored the other students.[14]

Finally, Hebrew University psychologist Ruth Butler showed how informational feedback is better than grades at both promoting kids' self-motivation to learn and boosting their achievement. Butler asked three groups of fifth- and sixth-graders to work on anagrams and two tasks from a creativity test. She graded the performance of one group, and gave written feedback on the strengths and weaknesses of their work to the second group. (For example, she said, "You thought of quite a few correct words; maybe it is possible to think of more long words.") The children in the third group received both grades and informational comments. After they had finished the work, the kids who received only comments performed best in the post test and also said they found the work more interesting than the other two groups of kids.[15]

Because grades are usually competitive, and not usually based on a student's personal progress, they rarely foster self-motivation to learn. Often they don't even promote more than minimal effort (just enough to stay out of trouble), since some kids know that even the most heroic try will not get them a good grade. Other kids aren't motivated to put out much effort because they know they can do well without exerting themselves.

Furthermore, grades rarely provide information about what your child knows or doesn't know. Even when they are based on the teacher's performance standards, they can be uninformative; standards usually vary greatly among teachers and even for different children in the same class.

To be more informative, some schools today are supplementing or replacing grades with descriptions of what children have learned. If your child's school doesn't give this useful information, I encourage you to ask for it.

Whatever your school's grading policy, you can influence your child's self-motivation tremendously by the way you treat her grades. The most important step you can take is not elevating them to the highest importance, which risks turning your child's attention away from learning and toward her As, Bs, Cs, and Ds.

Here are some other ways to keep grades from turning your child off to learning:

- Encourage your child to focus on short-term goals more than on grades: writing a good book report, learning more spelling words, or understanding the concepts he is studying in math.

I have known many parents who were shocked and angry when their child did very poorly on a standardized test after years of good grades. This is especially common in schools that serve predominantly low-income children, where some teachers develop low expectations, and therefore give inflated grades.

- When your child gets a report card, emphasize the teacher's comments and other information about what your child has learned. "You must feel proud of this report card" is fine; "You must feel proud of the progress you've made in math!" is even better.
- After your child takes a test, ask her, "Did you feel prepared? What kind of questions were there?" rather than "What grade did you get?"
- When she gets a good report card, resist the urge to run to the phone and call Grandma and Grandpa. Instead, acknowledge your child's accomplishment. "These grades are good. I can tell you really worked hard this grading period. You must be proud of yourself." Tell your relatives later how hard your child is working and how much she's learned.[16]

The more you can focus your child on the inherent pleasure of learning rather than on grades, the better. The more attention you give to internal rewards for studying—like the feelings of personal satisfaction and pride from a job well done—the less your child will depend on external stimuli like grades.

If your child's friends often compare grades, stay firm. Tell your child that what counts is the effort he puts into his work, and what he learns. If he knows that's what you care about, rather than how his grades stack up to his friends', that will go a long way toward erasing his worries about grade differences.

"But what about my child's self-esteem?" you might ask. "Won't rewards and good grades make her feel good about herself?" We'll examine that commonly held belief in the final chapter.

10

What's Self-Esteem Got to Do with It?

Six-year-old Joanna, "student of the day," stands on a table while her classmates applaud. Afterwards, the Self-Esteem Bunny, who is leading the workshop, gently lifts the little girl to the floor and leads her back to her seat. Joanna picks up her pencil and opens a workbook to its first page. "I am Joanna," she writes in her workbook. "I love and approve of myself."

Activities like this PTA-sponsored workshop were not uncommon after the self-esteem movement entered schools in the 1960s. Educators and parents hoped that making students feel good about themselves would spur them to higher academic achievement and even keep them away from gangs and drugs.

Today most of the most extreme examples of the self-esteem craze are disappearing. I hear less and less about self-esteem programs in schools, and of kids applauded "just for being me." But confusion about the role of self-esteem in children's academic lives persists. Perhaps your child has received a trophy for not doing much of anything, or has been urged to tell himself, for no particular reason, "I'm special." Maybe you've wondered occasionally, as I have, whether you should hold back criticism of your child or ignore a mistake she's made, because you don't want her to "feel bad about herself."

As parents, we're called upon almost daily to make these kinds of judgments. While the self-esteem movement rightly counsels us to consider our children's feelings, distortions and abuses of the self-esteem notion have also sown a great deal of confusion over the past twenty-five years, and made parents' decisions about praise and criticism all the more difficult.

Let's start unraveling the confusion about self-esteem with a brief look at why educators and parents alike became so concerned about children's feelings about themselves.

Where Did the Self-Esteem Movement Come From?

When I was in fourth grade in the late 1950s, I had an excellent teacher with an unfortunate flaw: when she was frustrated, Miss B. let off steam by mocking children who made mistakes or didn't catch on quickly. Screaming sarcastically, she called them "clunks" in front of the whole class. Years later, I realized how severely she'd hurt many classmates when one of them made a beeline for me at our twentieth high school reunion. Did I remember how Miss B. had called him a clunk? he asked, his face searching mine for confirmation. Yes, I remembered. "Wasn't that awful?" said Ed, relieved to have his terrible memories confirmed. "I've never forgotten it."

Miss B.'s brand of punishment—shaming and harsh criticism—was once fairly common. People thought that when children feared such remarks they would work hard to avoid them. In the early postwar years, American school discipline was not so far removed from old-time methods, such as sitting a child in the corner with a dunce cap on his head, or rapping his knuckles with a ruler.

Indeed, parenting experts earlier in the century were so far from cherishing children's tender feelings that they advised parents not to pick them up when they cried. In his 1928 book *Psychological Care of Infant and Child* (which included a chapter called "Too Much Mother Love"), the behavioral psychologist John Watson told parents not to "spoil" their children with affection. "Never hug and kiss them, never let them sit in your lap," he said. "If you must, kiss them once on the forehead when they say good night. Shake hands with them in the morning."[1]

These were the days of "Spare the rod and spoil the child."

Those beliefs in cool and punitive rigidity started changing in the early 1950s, as psychologists zeroed in on the importance of feelings about the self. Carl Rogers, for example, told parents to give their children "unconditional positive regard." The influential pediatrician Benjamin Spock, trained in child psychiatry, advised parents to trust their instincts and not to worry about "spoiling" a baby by responding lovingly to her needs and feelings. Brandeis University psychologist Abraham Maslow said that after basic survival and safety, self-esteem—a sense of oneself as a loved and valued human being—ranks highest among basic human needs.[2]

Soon psychologists began to appreciate the powerful link between children's feelings about themselves and their motivation to learn. Humiliation and fear of punishment, they realized, do far more harm than good. Fear leads to anger and withdrawal, not to increased effort.

The concept of self-esteem entered the educational mainstream in 1962, when the Association for Supervision and Curriculum Development, widely respected among educators, published an anthology devoted to the importance of self-esteem in a child's education. This volume remains the ASCD's most popular publication. Educators and parents began to think about how a child's feelings about himself affect his ability to learn. "Positive feedback" and praise became the order of the day in many classrooms and homes.

Efforts to use fear to motivate students certainly haven't vanished entirely. My friend Elizabeth, who lives in a school district with an excellent reputation, was distraught when her son, a hardworking fourth-grader who had done well on all his assignments and tests, brought home a report card full of Cs. David was crushed. The teacher told Elizabeth she'd given her son Cs to "motivate him to improve" during the next grading period. But David wasn't motivated to learn; he was discouraged and angry.

Overkill

Self-esteem was soon a buzzword. In many respects the self-esteem movement was healthy, because it undercut ideas about "motivating" children with threats and punishment. It emphasized instead the importance of encouragement, optimism, and positive feedback. It encouraged parents to give children a sense of personal worthiness, and of confidence that others will love and accept them for who they are.

But the pendulum swung too far. Self-esteem became a pixie dust that we could sprinkle over children to turn them into eager learners. "Positive self-esteem," parents were told repeatedly by the media, "is the best building block for success in school."[3] Jumping on the bandwagon, advertisers claimed that a certain cereal, the right toothpaste, new bedroom furniture, or a Hallmark card would inject children with the magic self-esteem elixir. (Revlon sponsored a school self-esteem lesson, which included an investigation of good and bad hair days.)[4] Persistence and achievement too often took a backseat to children "feeling good about themselves." As Carol Dweck remembers, a lot of people started thinking that "if you puff up someone's self-esteem, he's set for life."

The Self-Esteem Myths

Certainly your child's feeling of worthiness, his sense that you love, value, and accept him, is very important. And surely both success and some praise for her efforts contribute to her self-esteem. But research has made it crystal clear that many of the self-esteem theories and programs of the 1960s and 1970s were misguided.

Let's look at some of the common distortions of self-esteem.

"PRAISE: THE MORE THE BETTER"

One of the most frequent mistakes is praising everything a child says or does, slathering on compliments for feats that required no effort, just to make him "feel good" about himself. As I noted in chapter 9, praise can be powerful. But overpraising weakens your credibility. "If everything is wonderful," says UES teacher Richard Cohen, "and the kid knows some things he does aren't wonderful, then he thinks the person giving the reinforcement either has very low expectations, or must not have any idea what a good job is."[5]

According to newspaper columnist D. L. Stewart, self-esteem has been translated into "competitive child-praising" in many American families:

First parent: "That's a beautiful painting you drew."

Second parent: "It's more than beautiful, it's exquisite. It probably should be hanging in the local art museum."

First parent: "Local art museum? Please. It should be hanging in the Louvre next to the work of Da Vinci."

Second parent: "Da Vinci? Compared to this painting the junk he drew should be for sale in front of abandoned gas stations."[6]

"MISTAKES AND CRITICISM ARE BAD"

The flip side of pouring on excessive superficial praise is ignoring all your child's academic mistakes. Certainly you do want to overlook some of them. No one can correct a mountain of errors at once. And imagine how frustrating it would be to read out loud if someone corrected every word you stumbled over or mispronounced.

But don't think pointing out *some* mistakes will harm your child's self-esteem. (As I pointed out in chapter 8, quite the opposite is true.) Simply balancing your negative feedback with a compliment, as I counseled in that same chapter, will prevent discouragement: "Your story really made me laugh," you might say. "You need to double-check your spelling, though." Likewise, don't be afraid to criticize your child on occasion. Just remember to mix in positive comments and suggestions for improvement.

Compare these two parents' techniques of dealing with their children's report cards:

CHRIS: Here's my report card, Dad.

DAD #1: What a wonderful report card! This deserves a night at the ballpark, with all you want to eat. You're so brilliant!

CHRIS: But I got an "unsatisfactory" for "listening and following directions." Mrs. Hancock said I talk too much in class.

DAD #1: Oh, don't pay any attention to that. Mrs. Hancock just doesn't appreciate your high spirits. I did notice a D in handwriting, but so what. No one needs handwriting any more.

CHRIS: Yeah, Mrs. Hancock is too picky.

SAMANTHA: Here's my report card, Dad.

DAD #2: Thanks. Hmmm, let's see here. Good grades in social studies and English. That's great, Sam! I know you put a lot of work into those subjects. You must be proud of yourself.

SAMANTHA: Yeah.

DAD #2: I see here there's a "needs improvement" for class behavior. What's that about?

SAMANTHA: Mrs. Hancock says I'm too much of a chatterbox in class.

DAD (*laughs*): It must run in the family. I remember getting marked down for talking too much in school too. But doesn't it make it hard to understand what the teacher is saying? Don't you think it might disturb the other kids?

SAMANTHA: Oh. Well, maybe.

DAD: Any thoughts about how you could work on this one?

SAMANTHA: I guess I could try to talk less in class.

DAD: Maybe talk more at recess.

SAMANTHA (*laughs*): Okay.

Chris's father isn't really building his son's good feelings about himself by accepting everything he does. Samantha's father, on the other hand, expresses his acceptance and trust, while encouraging her to respond to the teacher's criticism. That's what fosters positive self-esteem.

"FAILURE IS BAD"

The need to protect children from failure is another common mistaken idea about self-esteem. Indeed, in chapter 8 I told you why failure is often productive. And remember the "just-right" challenge discussed in chapter 4, which takes your child to the next step in learning? If she regularly faces challenges, she's bound to fail sometimes. Occasional difficulty means she's stretching herself and maximizing her learning.

Failure will also harm your child's self-esteem if she thinks your approval of her depends on her success. That won't happen if instead of criticizing your child, you criticize her problem behaviors. For example, instead of "I'm disappointed in *you*," criticize the behavior behind the failure: "I'm disappointed that you watched TV last night instead of studying for your spelling test." Or even better, address the remedy: "I hope you'll study instead of watching TV the night before your next spelling test." While calling children "lazy," "stupid," or "bad" conveys disapproval of who they *are*, not of how they have behaved, even calling your child "smart," "creative," or "good" can disturb a child if she believes that your respect depends on the achievements that won her such praise.

"SELF-ESTEEM IS GETTING WHAT YOU WANT"

One day the well-known early childhood expert Lilian Katz visited a first-grade classroom, where she saw children putting together booklets entitled "All about Me." On each page the children had filled in information under titles such as "What I like to eat," "What I like to watch on TV," "What I want for a present," and "Where I want to go on vacation."

Katz was dismayed. Why weren't there pages in the children's booklets headed "What I am curious about," "What I want to make," or "What I want to explore, solve, or figure out"? she wondered. Why was the children's attention turned so insistently on their desires?[7]

Too many school activities, says Katz, confuse self-esteem with this kind of trivial self-celebration. "Feeling competent and worthy," she says, "isn't the same as having your needs and wishes gratified." The booklets, she concluded, confused self-esteem with narcissism.[8]

So don't be lured by advertisements telling you that buying your child a particular brand of clothes, candy, or tennis shoes will improve his self-esteem. In our affluent culture, it's easy to confuse giving your child a healthy personal sense of value with buying her an object of value. But make no mistake: getting your child the Power Ranger toy or baseball cap he's been whining for won't make him feel good about himself.

Beyond Self-Esteem

The relaxed and loving atmosphere created when your child knows you love and approve of her is critical to healthy emotional development and a love of learning. Feeling that your love doesn't depend on his school performance, your child can take risks and seek help. He can learn playfully, become increasingly competent, and feel solidly autonomous, all the while never losing his close link to you. Unworried about having to look smart, he can work hard and strive, taking on the "just-right" challenge.

If you follow the general outline of the mountain of advice I've given throughout this book, you will raise a child who works hard. She will make mistakes and meet obstacles, but persist to overcome them, and finally succeed, gaining new skills and understanding. That success will make your child confident, cheerful, optimistic, and energetic, and these good feelings about herself will spur her on to accomplish more.

As this cycle repeats itself many times over, your child will feel satisfied, knowing that he's developed his capability to the fullest, and that he's stretched and grown and perhaps even contributed to the community. This is a cycle that may even lead to a burst of creative energy that produces a dazzling painting, the answer to a tough math brain twister, or a speech delivered before the whole school. It's a psychological outlook that will allow your child to rewrite a book report three times, plunge into despair, and rewrite twice more until it finally reads right. "Darn, that's good!" she might tell herself. And after finishing a particularly demanding or creative project, she'll feel supremely satisfied and may even have moments of joy.

That is when she will realize that she loves learning.

APPENDIX:

CHOOSING A SCHOOL THAT WILL PROMOTE YOUR CHILD'S LOVE OF LEARNING

How can you choose the best preschool or elementary school for your child? Many parents don't have this luxury, but if you are in the enviable position of having a choice, how can you tell which school will promote a love of learning in your child? You can learn something about a school from other parents, and glean information about the school's values from its brochure, but the best way to pick a school—and the way I strongly recommend—is to visit it.

FINDING A PLAYFUL PRESCHOOL

Let's start thinking about your choice by visiting two very different preschools together:

Outside in California's January springtime, a troop of four-year-olds giggle as they blow dish soap mixed with sugar water into huge, shimmering bubbles bulging from a hollow plastic wand. Waiting her turn, a little girl jumps up and down with excitement. Two boys shriek happily, chasing a pink bubble as it floats across the yard. A teacher's aide keeps up a stream of descriptions and questions: "Why do you think they float in the air for so long?" she asks. "That one is gigantic!" she cries, and "Look at how they shimmer!"

Inside the nearby classroom, three girls sit at a small table sorting shapes varying in size and color. Across the room, a teacher's aide reads a story to a child on her lap, as four others crowd around her on the floor.

What on earth are these kids learning? Knowing how to blow bubbles probably won't plump up their SAT scores. But talking with the aide about the bubbles builds the children's vocabulary; taking turns with the wand-blower teaches them how to cooperate. And the game piques their scientific curiosity, prompting questions like "Why do all the bubbles come out round?" and "What makes them pop?"

Compare this scene to another at a different kind of preschool:

Twenty four-year-olds sit in a circle facing the teacher. They recite the alphabet, and then count to thirty. Next the teacher holds up a flash card, and the children call out the letter on the card in unison. The teacher completes the lesson by pulling down a map of the state and inviting a child to come up and point to the dot representing the city where the children live.

"Extraordinary!" you might think after visiting this second school. "They are so competent at such a young age!"

Not really. Young children often recite words without understanding the concepts behind them. The same child who can count to thirty may not be able to tell you how many cookies he'd have if he had two and you gave him one more. For him, counting to thirty is a string of sounds with no meaning. He may recognize the letters of the alphabet, but not realize that the letters on the flash cards are the stuff of which words, sentences, and stories are made. The state map has no more meaning to the girl who can locate Cincinnati on it than computer program codes or inflections in the Chinese language have to me.

Rather than learning facts and symbols without understanding them, kids in preschool should learn chiefly through direct experience—what educators sometimes call "hands-on" learning. Good preschools guide children through the same kinds of playful learning activities that I recommend to parents in chapter 2.

Some parents believe that teaching basic academic skills in preschool is necessary to give their kids a competitive edge. They may insist on formal teaching because they want to "create" a gifted child, to send their child to a prestigious private high school or an Ivy League college, or to ensure the academic success that will bring them "badges of good parenting," to borrow a phrase from Los Angeles psychologist Wendy Mogel. For other families, early learning seems like a way to bridge social and economic inequities, or to get a head start in today's competitive job market. And then there are parents who demand preschool academics because they mistakenly believe that the exciting new brain research calls for it, or because they want to assuage their guilt about leaving their children while they work.

My research has found that formal academic teaching for preschoolers, like that in the second school I describe above, can do more than waste their time: a strong emphasis on formal basic skills can harm children's desire to learn. In one study, for example, my colleagues and I examined two types of classrooms for four-year-olds. In the first, "highly structured" type, the teacher taught formal lessons, for example, having children recite the alphabet, count, answer simple factual questions, and complete worksheets. In the second type of classroom, the teachers allowed students to choose among activities that helped them learn through play and concrete experiences. Typically these teachers set up several "activity centers" (like Jeff and Gabe's post office described in chapter 2, or the bubble blowing at the beginning of this chapter) for children to choose from. As the children played, the teachers moved around the room engaging children in conversation and making suggestions to guide their learning.

The more formal classes, we found, tended to dampen children's motivation to learn. Kids in highly structured preschools, on average, had less self-confidence in their academic ability, picked easier activities when given a choice, and showed less pride in their accomplishments than the kids in the more play-like classrooms.[1] The children in the more formal academic programs were also less independent than the other children, and said they worried more about school. (Other researchers have found that children in tightly structured preschool programs showed more anxiety symptoms like nail biting and tearing up worksheets than did kids in more play-like classrooms.)[2] In contrast, the four-year-olds in the playful classrooms were more self-confident and more willing to take academic risks, and showed more pride in their work.

In a second study, we observed the two different kinds of classrooms for a half day each and found that discipline was more of a problem in the formal academic preschools.[3] Repeatedly, we saw scenes like this:

> Jake is supposed to be writing rows of the letter *B* on a paper with solid and dotted lines. After writing one row, he gets up to play with Legos on the rug. "We're writing *B*s now, Jake," the teacher gently reminds him. Jake obediently returns to his desk. But after writing only a few more letters, he goes back to the Legos. With each return trip to the table, the teacher's voice grows harsher, until finally Jake is sent to the "time out" chair.

Jake is not a defiant little boy. He's simply bored with work that is meaningless to him. Indeed, our research found that kids in tightly structured programs got into trouble far more than those in the more play-like classrooms. We think this happens because the children in the more formal classrooms don't enjoy or see much value in their work.

But kids in the playful classrooms approach their activities eagerly because they choose them and because they enjoy using hands-on objects like beads and wooden shapes, and materials like clay, paint, and paste. The students are also enthusiastic because the activities are flexible and therefore, as I explain in chapter 2, "just right" for advancing each child's understanding and skills and making children feel proud and confident.

Look for Kids Learning Basic Skills through Play

If you want your child to love learning, find a preschool or day care program where teachers create a world of learning through play. A good teacher will set up activities that will interest your child and at the same time teach her the skills she needs to succeed in elementary school.

You should see students choosing from among different projects. The teacher might be guiding their learning as she moves from child to child, by focusing children's attention ("Look at the color the paint became when you mixed the red and yellow!"), asking questions ("What color do you think mixing red and blue will make?"), or giving suggestions ("Why don't you try to paint your name at the bottom of the picture?"). She should be helping each child take the next step, the one he needs to take to develop his skills. If she sees a child wandering, she may take his hand and ask, "Which activity would you like to go to?"

The social trend toward early academics is not new. In 1885, leading American psychologist G. Stanley Hall warned of the "grave danger" posed by late-Victorian parents who, "perhaps not without vanity and cupidity, not only allow but sometimes encourage teachers to over-press their children, and sow seeds of suffering and incapacity."[4]

Good early childhood teachers also plan group activities with clear learning goals in mind. They may take children on a nature walk and encourage them to classify the leaves they collect by color, shape, or even the type of tree. They might organize muffin baking, pointing out the different sizes of measuring cups as the students use them, and even sneak in a little lesson by asking, "How many half cups of water will fill up a whole cup?"

As she reads a story, the teacher should ask questions to help kids develop analytic and verbal skills. She will help them understand emotions and relationships by nudging them to connect stories to their own lives: "Have any of you ever known a bully? Lost a pet? Moved to a new school?" Hands shoot up, and the teacher guides the ensuing conversation, helping her students describe their own experiences and feelings and listen to those of others.

Skilled teachers connect to children's interests when they teach, as I once saw a brilliant kindergarten teacher do during a lesson on measurement. In the midst of the discussion, a child volunteered that she was wearing new shoes. The teacher immediately turned the student's shoe into a measurement device. Capitalizing on the other children's interest in the girl's new shoes, she kept her students riveted while introducing the idea that any object can serve as an instrument of measurement.

Don't be alarmed if a preschool classroom is a bit noisy, or if the kids move around a lot and seem to play all day. Orderly youngsters sitting quietly at desks working with pencils and paper are not good signs. Kids shouldn't be screeching at the top of their lungs or wrestling on the floor. Order and discipline should prevail. But activities that look frivolous may be teaching important concepts, because the really good teacher plants lessons in all activities.

On the other hand, you want to make sure the school doesn't romanticize play. Just because an activity is fun doesn't mean it is educational. I often see preschoolers, for example, painting macaroni and pasting them on to paper. Teachers have explained to me that the activity teaches math concepts. It could, if the teacher structured it to focus children's attention on numbers, asking, for example, "How many blue macaroni do you have?" "How many red?" and "Do you have more blue or more red macaroni?" But without teacher guidance, the activity is mostly about painting and pasting, not math.

Examine carefully what children are doing. If it's not obvious, ask the teacher what she expects them to learn from the activity. She should be able to explain the learning goals clearly. Then think about whether the activity teaches children those lessons. Judge yourself whether any learning is actually going on. Play is romanticized at some schools, and the prohibition against formal teaching can be so strong that teachers are reluctant even to weave lessons into playful activities. You want teachers who are concerned about children's academic skill acquisition as well as their love of learning.

Are All Paper and Pencil Activities Bad?

Most preschool education experts frown on flash cards and worksheets. That's because preschoolers generally learn better, and in a deeper and longer-lasting way, when they manipulate hands-on materials, and when learning is linked to their own interests and experience.

But like any rule, this one must be applied flexibly. Paper and pencil tasks are not inherently bad for kids, and some children enjoy them. Good teachers, like good parents, respond to the needs and interests of individual children. A high-quality school may have flash cards or worksheets available for children who like them. What's important is not forcing young children to spend hours on activities they don't enjoy. It's a steady diet of boring exercises that takes away their appetite for learning.

What about Reading?

Beware of preschool programs that promise to teach reading. Many parents know—and the research has clearly shown—that children who haven't learned to read by the end of third grade usually have serious academic difficulties later on. But preschool is usually too early for formal reading instruction.

Research shows that teaching reading directly at an early age neither speeds up the development of reading skills nor predicts better reading later on.[5] There's no advantage to teaching a child to read with difficulty at age four when she'll learn far more quickly and comfortably at five or six. If your child is forced to learn to read before she's ready, she's likely to think reading is something she has to do to please you or the teacher rather than something she wants to do for pleasure.

There are, of course, exceptions. Some precocious children are ready and eager to learn to read at age four. You'll know if you have one. She'll ask you about letters and words, and try to sound them out herself. A sensitive preschool teacher will help her with the basics of reading, or you can do the same when she asks you and when she's obviously enjoying it.

A good preschool will do a lot, however, to prepare children to read. Research has shown, for example, that bathing children in experiences and language during the first five years (as I describe in chapters 2 and 3) promotes reading skills most effectively.[6] The larger vocabulary that kids gain in high-quality preschools and day care is especially important preparation for reading, since using phonics to decode letters is much easier when a child recognizes the word she's decoding.

Indeed, a recent national study of day care programs showed that the richness of the language environment strongly predicted children's language and other intellectual skills. With funding from the National Institute of Child Health and Human Development (NICHD), researchers studied 1,364 kids spread across the nation. They visited the children at home and at child care, and tested their sentence complexity at age two and their spoken and understood vocabulary at age three. Those children whose caregivers held conversations with them, the study found, had larger vocabularies, used more complex sentences, and understood more than the kids in lower-quality, less language-rich care.

So pay particular attention to the use of language at a preschool or day care program. Watch how the adults talk to kids. Do they have conversations with them, or simply give orders? Is there a lot of story reading and storytelling? Do children learn rhymes and songs that are meaningful to them? Are they asked to share, explain, and elaborate on their thoughts? These are the signs of an environment that will prepare your child to become a skilled and eager reader.

When you are visiting the school, notice too whether teachers are "teaching" as they read stories, not simply reading them. They may point out letters in words that are the same as the first letter of one of the student's names. Or they may use "big books" and ask the children to find all the Ms on a page. Perhaps you will see a teacher read a book on animals and then start a game of thinking up animal names that start with an s sound.

Although phonics is a critical component of reading, good readers can also analyze what they have read, make comparisons, and check their own understanding. Effective teachers promote thinking about a story by asking children questions like "Why do you think Arnold felt so sad?" or "Where do you think the zookeeper will find the lion?" You may see the teacher point to pictures in the book—"See, there's the birthday cake that Sally's mother surprised her with"—to teach children to look for clues to understanding a story.

Preschools and day care centers should also have plenty of books that children can look at on their own. They should be varied, including some picture books and some books with one or two simple words that a child can begin to read when she's ready.

Children's knowledge of the world also contributes to their reading skills. Look for a program that takes field trips and plans activities that provide the rich experiences I recommend for your child in chapters 1 and 2. A story about a panda means far more to a child who has seen one at the zoo; a child who has watched his friend's mother cook latkes, spring rolls, or tortillas at school has a head start for studying world cultures, history, or a foreign language. Don't choose a school that parks children in front of television or allows them to play endlessly with the same toys.

And avoid, if you can, a preschool where the teacher tells the kids exactly what to do and how to do it most of the day. Instead find (or work with other parents to start) one that gives your child choices and nurtures your child's natural desire to understand the world through playful activities, starting him on the path to a lifetime of loving learning.

SHOULD I WAIT A YEAR TO PUT MY YOUNG CHILD IN KINDERGARTEN?

Many parents are faced with the dilemma of whether to enroll a relatively young child in kindergarten or to hold him out for a year. Parents of boys who have birthdays just before the kindergarten cutoff date are the most likely to opt for a delay, reasoning that the extra year of social, intellectual, and physical maturity will help their child succeed in school. This practice, sometimes called "red-shirting," has become so widespread that it is estimated that as many as 10 percent of American children enter kindergarten a year late.

But while a few studies have found that the oldest children in a kindergarten class do a bit better than the youngest children, the small advantage, when it is found, usually disappears by the third grade. Furthermore, in the study I conducted of children from kindergarten through the third grade, at no grade did teachers rate their youngest students any less socially or academically competent than the oldest children in their classes.[7]

I can't say whether *your* child will benefit from waiting an extra year to start kindergarten, because research tells us only how a practice affects children *on average*. Some children may benefit from waiting a year before starting kindergarten. But the research is very clear—"red-shirting" is highly overrated. It doesn't give most kids the advantage their parents expect. And for many kids, starting school when they are eligible will contribute more to their intellectual and social development than staying home or in day care another year.

CHOOSING AN ELEMENTARY SCHOOL

Fourth- and fifth-graders in groups of three or four are hunched over computers distributed around the classroom. One student in each group types in questions about the body posed by the other children: "How does poison affect the body?" "What is the function of hemoglobin?" "How do cigarettes affect your lungs?"

The teacher moves from group to group, helping children to clarify their questions and choose one to pursue in depth. Once each group has selected its question, the children will consult classroom references and books checked out of the school library. They'll search for information on the Web, and e-mail experts. The teacher will provide ongoing assistance and suggestions. Occasionally, she will teach a formal lesson about human physiology, or about strategies for finding, evaluating, and summarizing information. Periodically the groups will make presentations on their progress, receiving feedback and suggestions from their classmates and the teacher. In their final report, they will use diagrams, photographs, computer simulations, and text to communicate what they have learned.

This snapshot shows a teacher using several strategies that promote children's enthusiastic participation while teaching them basic academic, planning, and social skills.

First, although the teacher gives some traditional instruction—as when she supplies background science information—students also ask questions they especially want answered. Thus she encourages their curiosity and individual interests.

Second, children have considerable autonomy. In addition to choosing (with the teacher's guidance) their question, they have some leeway in how they organize and do their report. As a result, they will feel ownership of both their product and their learning.

Third, rather than passively listening to the teacher or reading a textbook, students are creating a multidimensional report. Their product will give them greater satisfaction and feelings of competence than would a more traditional task, such as answering a page of short-answer, factual questions.

Fourth, rather than repeating the same assignment—like reading textbook chapters—the children are engaging in a variety of complex activities.

Fifth, the assignment is flexible, allowing each child to contribute by taking on a "just-right" challenge. For example, each student can examine an information source that matches her reading level. And the project can be broken up into pieces, so that each member of a group does a task that he is able to complete, but also requires him to develop his skills and understanding.

Sixth, the children work collaboratively, which enhances their enjoyment as well as their communication and other social skills.

Finally, the teacher and the other students give each group periodic feedback, which helps students improve their report. The frequent and substantive evaluation focuses their attention on the learning goal at hand ("This is what I need to do to do a good job"), rather than on performance ("I need to do this to get an A").

This is the kind of elementary school teaching and learning activity that will enhance your child's joy in learning while giving her the skills and knowledge she needs to succeed in school.

Questions to Ask at a School Visit

But how can you tell whether the schools you're considering provide such a program? Here are some questions to ask administrators or teachers to help you make that judgment:

1. How are children evaluated?
Grades alone are not enough. Teachers should give children frequent and useful feedback to guide their efforts. For example, when

children are asked to write, they should get more than a grade or a score back from the teacher. They also need comments on what was good about their writing, and what they should work on. The feedback should focus the student's attention on improvement or achieving a well-specified set of skills rather than comparing him with other students.

Even kids who are doing better than most of their classmates should get constructive criticism. *All* students need information both about the competencies they have achieved and how they can improve their skills.

2. *When and how do you give parents information about student progress?*

If your child is going to be competent and have confidence in his ability to succeed in school, you need to know when he needs extra help or encouragement. A school should give you specific information on your child's academic strengths and weaknesses, based on a clear standard. Letter grades alone won't give you this information.

The teacher should tell you how your child is doing within a few months after school begins, and update you again well before the end of the year. This timing will allow you to help your child as soon as problems emerge, and well before the year is over.

3. *How do you individualize work to ensure that it's appropriately difficult for each student?*

Many elementary schools group children by ability in an effort to match instruction to children's skill levels. Ability grouping is effective and won't undermine children's motivation if it is flexible, meaning that children are frequently reassessed and change groups when appropriate. Teachers should also attend to the skill differences among children in a group.

Cooperative learning groups, in which each child does a part of the

Once I visited a middle school I was considering for my daughter where the head of the school repeated the word "excellence" over and over in his presentation. It made me wonder whether children ever had a chance to "muck about"—to simply enjoy developing a new skill without having to worry about excelling. College preparation and admissions were also discussed at great length. But nothing was said about the seventh-grade curriculum. I am just as concerned about Meredith attending a good college as any parent. But she was only eleven years old at the time, and I didn't want college admission to be the only goal of her middle school education. I walked out before the classroom visits, and saved money by having one less application fee to pay.

project that is geared to her skill level, can provide another way to ensure that children are appropriately challenged. (For an explanation of cooperative learning, see chapter 8.)

A good teacher will also assign work that all students do (to avoid stigmatizing some children), but that each child can complete according to her own skill level. For example, the entire class might have the same writing assignment, but one child will write a longer and more complex essay than another. Even math problems can be solved at different levels. For example, one child might multiply 4×3 by using addition and adding up three, four times. Another child might draw groups of three dots and then count the dots, or use buttons the teacher gives him to do the same thing. Still another child might count up "dots" in her head, while her friend uses a memorized math fact, $4 \times 3 = 12$. These children are using different levels of mathematical understanding to solve the same problem.

4. How do teachers measure children's skills to decide what they need to learn next?

Standardized test scores are not very useful for gauging children's individual teaching needs. To provide children with appropriately challenging work, teachers should frequently assess very specific skills, check children's written assignments, and observe them carefully in class. Good teachers should be able to describe several different ways they evaluate children's skills and understanding.

5. How does the school promote children's curiosity and creativity?

Look for work that allows children to ask their own questions and develop their own thinking. Writing assignments shouldn't be limited to copying sentences, adding punctuation, or answering factual questions. Children should also learn to generate their own sentences and paragraphs, and they should be given opportunities to write about topics that interest them. Teachers also might ask students to make up their own math problems, or to find different strategies for solving them. They can encourage children to connect a social studies lesson to their own lives, or to make up their own science questions, like the children studying human physiology at the beginning of this section.

6. Do children have opportunities to collaborate with peers?

In some schools, help from other students is considered cheating. But in classrooms that promote a love of learning, teachers realize that children enjoy working together, and when one child helps another, both can benefit (see chapter 8).

7. Can you describe some examples of school assignments that require children to learn "hands on" or in other active ways?

Children seldom get excited about listening to a lecture, reading from a textbook, or filling out worksheets. They are more likely to be deeply engaged when they are actively involved in learning. For example, reading authentic letters written during the American Civil War and then writing to a pretend brother fighting on the other side is more interesting than reading in a textbook about families divided by the war. Building an experimental volcano will stimulate a child more than simply reading about one. Learning how to create and read bar graphs is more absorbing when children make graphs based on their own survey of classmates' favorite ice cream flavors than when they complete a set of worksheet problems. Teachers should be able to give many examples of such activities.

8. How much choice do children get in their schoolwork?
Children should have some choice both in what assignments they do and how they do them. For example, children should have some opportunities to choose from among several books for reading assignments. They should sometimes be allowed to pick their writing topics. A good teacher might even encourage students to select their own vocabulary words from those they don't understand in a book they are reading, or to choose among computer programs for developing fluency in math. Art projects, too, should allow originality and imagination.

Keep Your Eyes Open
You can learn a great deal by looking at classrooms. If desks are in rows, all facing the teacher, you may be in a classroom in which the teacher directs and monitors students' every move. Desks organized in groups or student chairs around tables usually mean that children work cooperatively and collaboratively.

A rug, pillows, and stuffed animals suggest that the teacher is trying to make learning comfortable and enjoyable. Think about it: would you enjoy reading a book sitting on a hard chair at a desk?

Student work displays can be very informative. Are all the papers identical? That would imply the teacher does not encourage individuality or creativity. Is the only evidence of teacher feedback a grade or score, or has the teacher given useful feedback? Is there any evidence of collaboration? Has the teacher displayed papers that show individual progress, or only those with 100 percent correct or an A (which, as I explained in chapter 8, suggests the teacher focuses on performance rather than on learning)?

Are there "hands-on" art and science materials, math "manipulatives" (like sticks and beads), computers, reference books, and maps? These kinds of resources allow children to explore and create. Is there an assortment of books students can read, or only sets of textbooks?

Look to see if children can have easy access to materials and equipment, with responsibility for returning them. If the things they need to complete assignments are locked up or out of reach, students can't function autonomously. They are dependent on the teacher, who consequently spends more time managing supplies than teaching.

If you visit on a school day, look at what the students are doing. Are they actively involved in their work or passively "going through the motions"? Is there a low hum, an occasional expression of enthusiasm? That's good—classrooms where you can hear a pin drop are not usually very exciting for children. What's important is that the conversations and other noise are related to the task at hand, not the result of unrelated conversations or "fooling around."

Look carefully at what they are learning. In some elementary schools, student enthusiasm is considered the hallmark of a good lesson. Enthusiasm is great, but not at the expense of learning. Just as I recommended for preschools, hone in on the learning when you visit an elementary school. If the purpose of an activity isn't obvious, the teacher should be able to clarify it for you.

Look, too, at what the teacher is doing. Is she lecturing or is she involving children in conversation? Is she asking questions that will plumb the students' understanding, so she can adjust the lesson if necessary, or that will challenge them to push their thinking to the next step? If teachers look aloof, or if they talk only about discipline and cleanup, this is not the school for your child.

These are my suggestions. But all the recommendations in this book

Once I watched a third-grade class cutting cardboard shapes to make into buildings, an activity the teacher claimed helped children develop basic geometry concepts. The kids were having a ball gluing, painting, and decorating boxes. At first glance, the project appeared engaging and potentially educational. But these children already knew how to cut and paste, and the activity continued for days. Perhaps 5 percent of the students' time was devoted to the mathematics involved.

apply to schools and teachers as well as to parents. So you have much more to look for when you visit schools than I was able to mention in this appendix.

Feelings of competence and autonomy, and secure, positive relationships between the teachers and staff and your child at school are just as important as they are between you and your child at home. Find a school that promotes these feelings if you can so that your child's school is your partner and not your adversary in promoting your child's love of learning.

NOTES

Introduction

1. Harter (1981); Harter, Whitesell, and Kowalski (1992).

Chapter 1: Encouraging Your Child's Love of Learning

1. Feynman (1985), p. 173.
2. Feynman (1985), p. 174.
3. Ryan, Connell, and Plant (1990).
4. Ryan and Stiller (1991).
5. Gottfried (1985).
6. Sweet, Guthrie, and Ng (1998).
7. Danner and Lonky (1981).
8. Fabes, Moran, and McCullers (1981); Utman (1997).
9. Martin V. Covington, interview by author, June 29, 1999.
10. Csikszentmihalyi (1993), p. 181.
11. Novak, Hoffman, and Yung (2000).
12. Brophy (1983); Brophy, Rohrkemper, Rashid, and Goldberger (1983).
13. Goodwin (1998).
14. Friedman (1989).
15. Nel Noddings, interview by author, July 7, 1999.
16. Du Pre and Du Pre (1997), p. 29.

17. Richard Cohen, interview by author, June 15, 1999.
18. Nel Noddings, interview by author, June 29, 1999.
19. Covington (1992).

Chapter 2: Loving Learning through Play

1. UES is UCLA's laboratory elementary school, of which Deborah Stipek has been director since 1991 and which both authors' children attended.
2. Piaget (1976), p. 17.
3. Bruner (1985).
4. Bruner (1985).
5. McCracken (2000).
6. Dye (1999).
7. Lütkenhaus (1984).
8. McCracken (2000).
9. Greenfield, Camaioni, Ercolani, Weiss, Lauber, and Perruchini (1994).
10. Eron (in press).
11. Erikson (1963), p. 212.
12. Lieberman (1993).
13. Jean B. Sanville, Ph.D., B.C.D., letter to author, December 10, 1993. Dr. Sanville is a psychoanalyst in Los Angeles.
14. Bruner (1985), p. 605.
15. Sacks (1999).
16. Sacks (1999).
17. Authors Guild (1999), p. 18.
18. Elkind (1999).
19. Petroski (1999).
20. Plato (1901).

Chapter 3: Nothing Motivates Children More Than Competence

1. Danner and Lonky (1981).
2. Harter (1974).
3. Hoff-Ginsberg (1991).
4. Ohanian (1994).
5. For more math activities, see Stenmark, Thompson, and Cossey (1986). This was published as an outgrowth of the Family Math course at the Lawrence Hall of Science, University of California, Berkeley.
6. Stenmark, Thompson, and Cossey (1986).
7. Calkins (1997).
8. Weinberger (1996); Hess and Holloway (1984).

Chapter 4: Feeling Competent

1. Bandura (1989), p. 1176.
2. Phillips (1984); Phillips and Zimmerman (1990).

3. Girls' lack of confidence has been widely documented by psychologists. See, for example, Maccoby (1998); also Maccoby and Jackling (1974).
4. Sharon Nelson–Le Gall, interview by author, April 26, 1995.
5. Bandura and Schunk (1981).
6. Parsons, Kaczala, and Meece (1982).
7. Barker and Graham (1987).
8. Wendy Mogel, interview by author, October 1, 1998.
9. Parsons, Kaczala, and Meece (1982).
10. Byler (2000).

Chapter 5: Autonomy

1. From a story told to me by Lucia Diaz, executive director, Mar Vista Family Center, Los Angeles, April 28, 1995.
2. Watson (1972).
3. Richard Ryan, interview by author, April 14, 1995.
4. Grolnick, Frodi, and Bridges (1984).
5. Deci, Nezlek, and Sheinman (1981).
6. DeCharms (1968).
7. Zuckerman, Porac, Lathin, Smith, and Deci (1978).
8. Grolnick and Ryan (1989). The quote is from Richard Ryan, interview by author, April 14, 1995.
9. Lewin, Lippitt, and White (1939).
10. Ed Lonky, interview by author, April 1995.
11. Boggiano, Flink, Shields, Seelbach, and Barrett (1993).
12. Much of the empowering language ideas and examples in the following three sections are based on the program and manual of the Mar Vista Family Center, Los Angeles.

Chapter 6: The Power of Your Caring Connection

1. Anecdote based on idea from Richard Ryan, interview by author, April 14, 1995.
2. Ryan, Stiller, and Lynch (1994).
3. Grolnick, Ryan, and Deci (1991).
4. Frodi, Bridges, and Grolnick (1985).
5. Ryan and Solky (1996), p. 255.
6. Richard Ryan, interview by author, April 14, 1995.
7. Ryan and Solky (1996).
8. Richard Ryan, interview by author, September 3, 1997.
9. Emotional coaching was invented by University of Washington researchers Lynn Fainsilber Katz, John Gottman, and Carole Hooven.
10. Lynn Fainsilber Katz, interview by author, February 1, 1995.
11. Based on exercise provided by Mar Vista Family Center manual.
12. Langress (1999), pp. 6–7; Louis Ignarro, interview by author, August 8, 2000.

13. Ryan and Solky (1996), p. 265.
14. Grolnick, Deci, and Ryan (1997).
15. Carol Jago, interview by author, August 15, 2000.
16. Chin (1999).

Chapter 7: Your Child Can "Get Smart" If She Works Hard

1. Dweck (1999).
2. Seligman (1995), pp. 2–3.
3. Licht and Dweck (1984).
4. Henderson and Dweck (1990).
5. Dweck (1975).
6. James Stigler, interview by author, ca. 1993.
7. Lyman (1999).
8. Stevenson and Stigler (1992).
9. Sandra Graham, interview by author, March 1993.
10. Schlender (2000).
11. Lyman (1999).
12. Curry (1997).
13. Cohen (1998). Italics in original.
14. Dweck (1999).
15. Terman (1916), pp. 91–92.
16. Hollingworth (1926), p. 71.
17. Steele and Aronson (1995).
18. Gould (1981).
19. Woo (1997).
20. Binet (1975), p. 105.

Chapter 8: Getting Smart or Looking Smart?

1. Dweck (1999), p. 151.
2. Schunk (1996).
3. Graham and Golan (1991).
4. Ames and Archer (1988).
5. Meece, Blumenfeld, and Hoyle (1988).
6. Peterson and Swing (1982).
7. Ryan, Gheen, and Midgley (1998).
8. Dweck (1999), p. 10.
9. Adapted from questions used in Ames and Archer (1987).
10. Videotapes provided by James Stigler, Department of Psychology, UCLA.
11. Hoffman (1999).
12. Petroski (1997).
13. Kaufman (1999).
14. Amabile (1982).

15. Linda Weissler, interview by author, April 13, 1997. Weissler is a teacher at Clover Avenue Elementary School in Los Angeles and a group leader at the UCLA History-Geography Project.
16. Johnson and Johnson (1989a).
17. Ames and Ames (1984).

Chapter 9: Rewards and Grades

1. Casady (1975).
2. Cohen (1973).
3. Alschuler (1968).
4. Lepper, Greene, and Nesbitt (1973).
5. Ames and Ames (1990).
6. Marty Covington, interview by author, August 1993.
7. Harter (1978).
8. Amabile, Hennessey, and Grossman (1986).
9. Amabile and Hennessey (1992).
10. Ryan, Mims, and Koestner (1983).
11. Cited in Amabile and Hennessey (1992), p. 54.
12. Cited in Amabile and Hennessey (1992), p. 54.
13. Grolnick and Ryan (1987).
14. Kage (1991).
15. Butler (1988).
16. Based on Mar Vista Family Center manual.

Chapter 10: What's Self-Esteem Got to Do with It?

1. Maier (1998).
2. Maslow (1987).
3. Weinhaus and Friedman (1993).
4. Borowski (1999).
5. Richard Cohen, interview by author, August 5, 1993.
6. Stewart (1999).
7. Katz (1993).
8. Lynn Fainsilber Katz, interview by author, February 1, 1995.

Appendix: Choosing a School That Will Promote Your Child's Love of Learning

1. Stipek, Feiler, Daniels, and Milburn (1995).
2. Burts, Hart, Charlesworth, Fleege, Mosley, and Thomasson (1992).
3. Stipek, Feiler, Byler, Ryan, Milburn, and Salmon (1998).
4. Cited in Zuckerman (1987).
5. Whitehurst and Lonigan (1998); Scarborough and Dobrich (1994).
6. Whitehurst and Lonigan (1998); Scarborough and Dobrich (1994).
7. Stipek and Byler (in press).

BIBLIOGRAPHY

Alschuler, A. (1968). How to increase motivation through climate and structure. (Working paper No. 8) Cambridge, MA: Harvard University, Graduate School of Education, Achievement Motivation Development Project.

Amabile, T. (1982). Children's artistic creativity: Detrimental effects of competition in a field setting. *Personality and Social Psychology Bulletin, 8 (3),* 573–78.

Amabile, T., and Hennessey, B. A. (1992). The motivation for creativity in children. In A. Boggiano and T. Pittman (Eds.), *Achievement and motivation: A social developmental perspective* (pp. 54–74). New York: Cambridge University Press.

Amabile, T., Hennessey, B., and Grossman, B. (1986). Social influences on creativity: The effects of contracted-for reward. *Journal of Personality and Social Psychology, 50,* 14–23.

Ames, C., and Ames, R. (1984). Goal structures and motivation. *Elementary School Journal, 85,* 39–52.

———. (1990). Motivation and effective teaching. In L. Idol and B. Jones (Eds.), *Educational values and cognitive instruction: Implications for reform* (pp. 247–71). Hillsdale, NJ: Lawrence Erlbaum Associates.

Ames, C., and Archer, J. (1987). Mothers' beliefs about the role of ability and effort in school learning. *Journal of Educational Psychology, 79,* 409–14.

———. (1988). Achievement goals in the classroom: Students' learning strategies and motivation processes. *Journal of Educational Psychology, 80,* 260–67.

Authors Guild. (1999). The pleasures and perils of the freelance life. *Authors Guild Bulletin,* summer.

Bandura, A. (1989). Human agency in social cognitive theory. *American Psychologist, 44,* 1175–84.

Bandura, A., and Schunk, D. (1981). Cultivating competence, self-efficacy, and intrinsic interests through proximal self-motivation. *Journal of Personality and Social Psychology, 41,* 586–98.

Barker, G., and Graham, S. (1987). Developmental study of praise and blame as attributional cues. *Journal of Educational Psychology, 79,* 62–66.

Binet, A. (1975). *Modern ideas about children.* Trans. S. Heisler. Menlo Park, CA: Suzanne Heisler, Publisher.

Boggiano, A., Flink, C., Shields, A., Seelbach, A., and Barrett, M. (1993). Use of techniques promoting students' self-determination: Effects on students' analytic problem-solving skills. *Motivation and Emotion, 17,* 319–36.

Borowski, J. (1999). Schools with a slant. *New York Times,* August 21.

Bowlby, J. (1973). Self-reliance and some conditions that promote it. In R. Gosling (Ed.), *Support, Innovation, and Autonomy.* London: Tavistock.

Brophy, J. (1983). Fostering student learning and motivation in the elementary school classroom. In S. Paris, G. Olson, and H. Stevenson (Eds.), *Learning and motivation in the classroom* (pp. 283–305). Hillsdale, NJ: Lawrence Erlbaum Associates.

Brophy, J., Rohrkemper, M., Rashid, H., and Goldberger, M. (1983). Relationships between teachers' presentations of classroom tasks and students' engagements in those tasks. *Journal of Educational Psychology, 75,* 544–52.

Bruner, J. (1985). On teaching thinking: An afterthought. In S. Chipman, J. Segal, and R. Glaser (Eds.), *Thinking and learning skills.* Vol. 2, *Research and open questions.* Hillsdale, NJ: Lawrence Erlbaum Associates.

Burts, D., Hart, C., Charlesworth, R., Fleege, P., Mosley, J., and Thomasson, R. (1992). Observed activities and stress behaviors of children in developmentally appropriate and inappropriate kindergarten classrooms. *Early Childhood Research Quarterly, 7,* 297–318.

Butler, R. (1988). Enhancing and undermining intrinsic motivation: The effects of task-involving and ego-involving evaluation on interest and performance. *British Journal of Educational Psychology, 58,* 1–14.

Byler, P. (2000). Middle school girls' attitude toward math and science: Does setting make a difference? Ph.D. dissertation, University of California, Los Angeles.

Calkins, L. (1997). *Raising lifelong learners: A parent's guide.* Reading, MA: Addison-Wesley.

Casady, M. (1975). The tricky business of giving rewards. *Psychology Today, 8,* 52.

Chin, D. (1999). Losing faith: School and the role of academics in the lives of immigrant students. Unpublished manuscript.

Cohen, H. (1973). Behavior modification in socially deviant youth. In C. Thoresen (Ed.), *Behavior Modification in Education: Seventy-Second Yearbook of the*

National Society for the Study of Education 72, Part 1, 291–314. Chicago, IL: University of Chicago Press.

Cohen, P. (1998). A woman's worth: 1857 letter echoes still. *New York Times,* July 18.

Covington, M. (1992). *Making the grade: A self-worth perspective on motivation and school reform.* New York: Cambridge University Press.

———. (1999). Caring about learning. The nature and nurturing of subject matter appreciation. *Educational Psychologist, 34,* 127–36.

Csikszentmihalyi, M. (1993). *The evolving self: A psychology for the third millennium.* New York: HarperPerennial.

Curry, J. (1997). Stepfather says Irabu is the son of an American. *New York Times,* July 15.

Danner, F., and Lonky, E. (1981). A cognitive-developmental approach to the effects of rewards on intrinsic motivation. *Child Development, 52,* 1043–52.

DeCharms, R. (1968). From pawns to origins: Toward self-motivation. In G. Lesser (Ed.), *Psychology and educational practice* (pp. 380–407). Glenview, IL: Scott, Foresman and Co.

Deci, E., Nezlek, J., and Sheinman, L. (1981). Characteristics of the rewarder and intrinsic motivation of the rewardee. *Journal of Personality and Social Psychology, 40,* 1–10.

Deci, E., and Ryan, R. (1987). The support of autonomy and the control of behavior. *Journal of Personality and Social Psychology, 53,* 1024–37.

Du Pre, H., and Du Pre, P. (1997). *Hilary and Jackie.* New York: Ballantine Books.

Dweck, C. (1975). The role of expectations and attributions in the alleviation of learned helplessness. *Journal of Personality and Social Psychology, 31,* 674–85.

———. (1999). *Self-theories: Their role in motivation, personality, and development.* Philadelphia: Psychology Press.

Dye, L. (1999). Researchers building robotic prototype, Lego block by Lego block. *Los Angeles Times,* September 6.

Elkind, D. (1999). The transformation of play in play, policy, and practice connections. *Newsletter of the Play, Policy & Practice Caucus of the National Association for the Education of Young Children, 4 (3),* 2.

Erikson, E. (1963). *Childhood and society.* New York: W. W. Norton.

Eron, L. (in press). Seeing is believing. In A. Bohart and D. Stipek (Eds.), *Constructive and destructive behavior: Implications for family, school, and society.* Washington, D.C.: American Psychological Association.

Fabes, R., Moran, J., and McCullers, J. (1981). The hidden costs of rewards and WAIS subscale performance. *American Journal of Psychology, 94,* 387–98.

Feynman, R. (1985). *"Surely you're joking, Mr. Feynman!"* New York: W. W. Norton.

Friedman, T. (1989). *From Beirut to Jerusalem.* New York: Farrar, Straus, and Giroux.

Frodi, A., Bridges, L., and Grolnick, W. (1985). Correlates of mastery-related behavior: A short-term longitudinal study of infants in their second year. *Child Development, 56,* 1291–98.

Goodwin, D. K. (1998). Life outside academe. *Key Reporter,* summer.

Gottfried, A. (1985). Academic intrinsic motivation in elementary and junior high school students. *Journal of Educational Psychology, 77,* 631–45.

Gould, S. (1981). *The mismeasure of man.* New York: W. W. Norton.

Graham, S., and Golan, S. (1991). Motivational influences on cognition: Task involvement, ego involvement, and depth of information processing. *Journal of Educational Psychology, 83,* 187–94.

Greenfield, P., Camaioni, L., Ercolani, P., Weiss, L., Lauber, B., and Perruchini, P. (1994). Cognitive socialization by computer games in two cultures: Inductive discovery or mastery of an iconic code? *Journal of Applied Developmental Psychology, 15,* 59–85.

Grolnick, W., Deci, E., and Ryan, R. (1997). Internalization within the family: The self-determination theory perspective. In J. Grusec and L. Kuczyhski (Eds.), *Parenting and children's internalization of values: A handbook of contemporary theory* (pp. 135–61). New York: John Wiley.

Grolnick, W., Frodi, A., and Bridges, L. (1984). Maternal control style and the mastery motivation of one-year-olds. *Infant Mental Health Journal, 5,* 72–82.

Grolnick, W., and Ryan, R. (1987). Autonomy in children's learning: An experimental and individual difference investigation. *Journal of Personality and Social Psychology, 52,* 890–98.

————. (1989). Parent styles associated with children's self-regulation and competence in school. *Journal of Educational Psychology, 81,* 143–54.

Grolnick, W., Ryan, R., and Deci, E. (1991). Inner resources for school achievement: Motivational mediators of children's perceptions of their parents. *Journal of Educational Psychology, 83,* 508–17.

Harter, S. (1974). Pleasure derived by children from cognitive challenge and mastery. *Child Development, 45,* 661–69.

————. (1978). Pleasure derived from challenge and the effects of receiving grades on children's difficulty level choices. *Child Development, 49,* 788–99.

Harter, S. (1981). A model of mastery motivation in children: Individual differences and developmental change. In W. Collins (Ed.), *Minnesota Symposium on Child Psychology, 14,* 215–55. Hillsdale, NJ: Lawrence Erlbaum Associates.

Harter, S. Whitesell, N., and Kowalski, P. (1992). Individual differences in the effects of educational transitions on young adolescents' perceptions of competence and motivational orientation. *American Educational Research Journal, 29,* 777–807.

Henderson, V., and Dweck, C. (1990). Achievement and motivation in adolescence: A new model and data. In S. Feldman and G. Elliot (Eds.), *At the threshold: The developing adolescent.* Cambridge, MA: Harvard University Press.

Hess, R., and Holloway, S. (1984). Family and school as educational institutions. *Review of Child Development Research, 7,* 179–222.

Hoff-Ginsberg, E. (1991). Mother-child conversation in different social classes and communications settings. *Child Development, 62,* 782–96.

Hoffman, J. (1999). Public lives; not exactly starting over: Writer's choices. *New York Times,* June 9.

Hollingworth, L. (1926). *Gifted children: Their nature and nurture.* New York: Macmillan.

Johnson, D., and Johnson, R. (1989a). *Cooperation and competition: Theory and research.* Edina, MT: Interaction Book Company.

———. (1989b). Toward a cooperative effort. *Educational Leadership, 46,* 80–81.

Kage, M. (1991). The effects of evaluation on intrinsic motivation. Paper presented at the meeting of the Japanese Association of Educational Psychology, Joetsu, Japan.

Katz, L. (1993). *Distinctions between self-esteem and narcissism: Implications for practice.* Urbana, IL: ERIC Clearinghouse on Elementary and Early Childhood Education.

Kaufman, J. (1999). Not exactly starting over: Writer's choices. *New York Times,* October 6.

Langness, D. (1999). From backyard rockets and hot rods to the Nobel Prize: The scientific journeys of Louis Ignarro. *UCLA Medicine Magazine,* summer.

Lepper, M., Greene, D., and Nesbitt, R. (1973). Undermining children's intrinsic interest with intrinsic rewards: A test of the overjustification hypothesis. *Journal of Personality and Social Psychology, 28,* 129–37.

Lewin, K., Lippitt, R., and White, R. (1939). Pattern of aggressive behavior in experimentally created "social climates." *Journal of Experimental Psychology, 10,* 271–99.

Licht, B., and Dweck, C. (1984). Determinants of academic achievement: The interaction of children's achievement orientations with skill area. *Developmental Psychology, 20,* 628–36.

Lieberman, A. (1993). *The Emotional life of the toddler.* New York: Free Press.

Lütkenhaus, P. (1984). Pleasure derived from mastery in three year-olds: Its function for persistence and the influence of maternal behavior. *International Journal of Behavioral Development, 7,* 343–58.

Lyman, R. (1999). A culture of both luck and pluck. *New York Times,* December 18.

Maccoby, E., and Jackling, C. (1974). *The psychology of sex differences.* Stanford, CA: Stanford University Press.

Maccoby, E. (1998). The two sexes: Growing up apart, coming together. Cambridge, MA: Belknap Press of Harvard University Press.

Maier, T. (1998). *Dr. Spock: An American life.* New York: Harcourt Brace.

Maslow, A. (1987). *Motivation and personality.* New York: Harper Collins.

McCracken, J. (2000). *Play is FUNdamental.* Washington, D.C.: National Association for the Education of Young Children.

Meece, J., Blumenfeld, P., Hoyle, R. (1988). Students' goal orientations and cognitive engagement in classroom activities. *Journal of Educational Psychology, 80,* 514–23.

Novak, T., Hoffman, D., and Yung, Y. (2000). Measuring the flow construct in online environments: A structural modeling approach. *Marketing Science,* winter 2000, 22–42.

Ohanian, S. (1994). *Garbage pizza, patchwork quilts, and math magic: Stories about teachers who love to teach and children who love to learn.* New York: W. H. Freeman.

Parsons, J., Kaczala, C., and Meece, J. (1982). Socialization of achievement attitudes and beliefs: Classroom influences. *Child Development, 53,* 322–39.

Peterson, P., and Swing, S. (1982). Beyond time on task: Students' reports of their thought processes during classroom instruction. *Elementary School Journal, 21,* 487–515.

Petroski, H. (1997). Designed to fail. *American Scientist, 85,* 416.

———. (1999). Work and play. *American Scientist, 87,* 208–12.

Phillips, D. (1984). The illusion of incompetence among academically competent children. *Child Development, 55,* 2000–2016.

Phillips, D., and Zimmerman, M. (1990). The developmental course of perceived competence and incompetence among competent children. In J. Kelligian and R. Sternberg (Eds.), *Competence considered* (pp. 41–66). New Haven, CT: Yale University Press.

Piaget, J. (1976). *The Child and reality: Problems of genetic psychology.* New York: Penguin Books.

Plato. (1901). *The Republic.* Book 7. R. Trans. B. Jowett. New York: Colonial Press.

Ryan, A., Gheen, M., and Midgley, C. (1998). Why do some students avoid asking for help? An examination of the interplay among students' academic efficacy, teachers' social-emotional role, and the classroom goal structure. *Journal of Educational Psychology, 90,* 528–35.

Ryan, R., Connell, J., and Plant, R. (1990). Emotions in nondirected text learning. *Learning and Individual Differences, 2,* 1–17.

Ryan, R., Mims, V., and Koestner, R. (1983). Relation of reward contingency and interpersonal context to intrinsic motivation: A review and test using cognitive evaluation theory. *Journal of Personality and Social Psychology, 45,* 736–50.

Ryan, R., and Solky, J. (1996). What is supportive about social support?: On the psychological needs for autonomy and relatedness. In G. Pierce, B. Sarason, and I. Sarason (Eds.), *Handbook of social support and the family* (pp. 249–67). New York: Plenum Press.

Ryan, R., and Stiller, J. (1991). The social contexts of internalization: Parent-teacher influences on autonomy, motivation and learning. *Advances in Motivation and Achievement, 7,* 138–39.

Ryan, R., Stiller, J., and Lynch, J. (1994). Representations of relationships to teachers, parents, and friends as predictors of academic motivation and self-esteem. *Journal of Early Adolescence, 14,* 226–49.

Sacks, O. (1999). Op-ed. *New York Times,* May 13.

Scarborough, H., and Dobrich, W. (1994). On the efficacy of reading to preschoolers. *Developmental Review, 14,* 245–301.

Schlender, B. (2000). $100 billion friendship. *Fortune,* October 25.

Schunk, D. (1996). Goal and self-evaluative influences during children's cognitive skill learning. *American Educational Research Journal, 33,* 359–82.

Seligman, M. (1995). *The Optimistic Child.* Boston, MA: Houghton Mifflin.

Seligman, M., and Maier, S. (1967). Failure to escape traumatic shock. *Journal of Experimental Psychology, 74,* 1–9.

Steele, C., and Aronson, J. (1995). Stereotype threat and the intellectual test performance of African Americans. *Journal of Personality and Social Psychology, 69,* 797–811.

Stenmark, J., Thompson, V., and Cossey, R. (1986). *Family math.* Berkeley: University of California.

Stevenson, H., and Stigler, J. (1992). *The learning gap.* New York: Summit Books/Simon and Schuster.

Stewart, D. L. (1999). Kids need to learn that life isn't fair. *Dayton (Ohio) Daily News,* June 7.

Stipek, D., and Byler, P. (in press). Academic achievement and social behaviors associated with age of entry into kindergarten. *Early Childhood Research Quarterly.*

Stipek, D., Feiler, R., Byler, P., Ryan, R., Milburn, S., and Salmon, J. (1998). Good beginnings: What difference does the program make in preparing young children for school? *Journal of Applied Developmental Psychology, 19,* 41–66.

Stipek, D., Feiler, R., Daniels, D., and Milburn, S. (1995). Effects of different instructional approaches on young children's achievement and motivation. *Child Development, 66,* 209–23.

Sweet, A., Guthrie, J., and Ng, M. (1998). Teacher perceptions and student reading motivation. *Journal of Educational Psychology, 90,* 210–23.

Terman, L. (1916). *The measurement of intelligence.* Boston: Houghton Mifflin.

Utman, C. (1997). Performance effects of motivational state: A meta-analysis. *Personality and Social Psychology Review, 1,* 170–82.

Watson, J. (1972). Smiling, cooing, and "the game." *Merrill-Palmer Quarterly, 18,* 323–40.

Weinberger, J. (1996). A longitudinal study of children's early literacy experiences at home and later literacy development at home and school. *Journal of Research in Reading, 19,* 14–24.

Weinhaus, E., and Friedman, K. (1993). Coping with kids. *Working Mother,* April.

Whitehurst, G., and Lonigan, C. (1998). Child development and emergent literacy. *Child Development, 69,* 848–72.

Woo, E. (1997). Education, not genetics a key IQ factor, study says. *Los Angeles Times,* November 12.

Zuckerman, M. (1987). Plus ça change: The high-tech child in historical perspective. *Early Childhood Research Quarterly, 2,* 255–64.

Zuckerman, M., Porac, J., Lathin, D., Smith, R., and Deci, E. (1978). On the importance of self-determination for intrinsically motivated behavior. *Personality and Social Psychology Bulletin, 4,* 443–66.

INDEX

ABOUT THE AUTHORS

DEBORAH STIPEK is dean of the School of Education at Stanford University. An internationally recognized scholar and researcher in the psychology of motivation, she directed for a decade UCLA's Corinne A. Seeds University Elementary School, known worldwide as a laboratory for innovation in instruction. She consults frequently on local and state educational policy, and chairs a MacArthur Foundation task force that seeks new ways to link scholarly research to school reform efforts. She lives in Palo Alto.

KATHY SEAL is a journalist and author who has written about education and psychology since 1985 for publications including *Family Circle, Parents*, and *The New York Times*, as well as for educators' magazines. She has also been a commentator on educational issues on Public Radio International's *Marketplace*. Kathy served for two years as copresident of the parent-teachers' association at UCLA's Seeds University Elementary School, the only laboratory elementary school in California. She and her husband Jim have two sons and live in Santa Monica.